AT HOME WITH THE INTERNET

Visit the At Home with the Internet website at:
www.homeinternetchannel.com

AT HOME
WITH
THE INTERNET

Matthew Smith

Hodder & Stoughton

First published in Great Britain in 2000 by Hodder and Stoughton
A division of Hodder Headline

10 9 8 7 6 5 4 3 2 1

A CIP catalogue record for this title is available from the British Library.

ISBN 0 340 76693 X

Printed and bound in Great Britain by
Mackays of Chatham PLC

Hodder and Stoughton
A division of Hodder Headline
338 Euston Road
London NW1 3BH

Contents

Internet Confidence
This section includes 3 easy guides which explain the basic Internet skills, in an easy, step-by-step way. These easy guides will give you the confidence to explore the Internet right away.

Internet Enjoyment
This section is packed full of advice and hints 'n' tips which will give you more enjoyment from your time on the Internet.

1
The Internet *Starts Here*

The first challenge I faced with the Internet was to find out how to get connected. Seeking the advice of some friends I soon had a connection to the Internet from my home computer. However, I began to realise that just having the Internet in my living room wasn't good enough. I wasn't using it. Not only did I need the basic skills of how to use the Internet, but I also wanted to find out how to have more fun with it!

I browsed through the Internet books and guides available but, unfortunately, I didn't get much help from them. They all seemed either to bog you down with jargon and technical stuff or just produce an endless list of websites to visit, none of which were relevant to me. I was getting fed up with the Internet pretty quickly.

My wish was simple enough. All I wanted was an easy-to-understand book that made the Internet fun for me. A book that provided bite-size pieces of information to help me get the most enjoyment from the Internet. No jargon, no endless pages of information, just a handy guide packed full of hints, tips and inspiration.

I soon discovered that there wasn't a book that wanted to build up my Internet confidence or was bothered to tell me how to have fun with it. So I wrote this one.

At Home with the Internet is for all those who find themselves in the same situation as I was. The book is written for *you*. It doesn't matter if you are just beginning with the Internet or if you have been using it for some time; you are sure to find something here to improve the time you spend on the Internet.

The book starts with a simple explanation of the basics to help you get going. The first three chapters are 'Easy Guides' to the most common skills and tools of the Internet. Kept jargon-free and simple, they will give you the confidence you need to find out what the Internet is all about. What's more, you can follow these guides at your own pace.

The 'Enjoying the Internet' section is full of interesting and fun things to do with the Internet, from getting a sneak preview of an upcoming movie to shopping for Internet bargains. Each page contains tips and hints for you to really start enjoying the Internet in your home.

Tip: Getting connected

Getting connected to the Internet has never been easier. More often than not, when you buy a new computer there is Internet connection advice already installed on it. Today's computers will also come with a built-in **modem**. A modem is the device that physically sets up the connection between your computer and the Internet.

Internet connection is also available from your telephone company or your local electronic and computer shops. I'm certain their staff will be able to give you the advice you need to link your computer to the Internet. Or do what I did and ask for some help from a friend, relative or work colleague who is already connected to the Internet.

Before you get started you may want to look at some of these very commonly asked questions.

What is the Internet?

Becoming Internet-confident starts with having some idea of what the Internet is.

There are many definitions of what the Internet is. The best one, in my opinion, describes the Internet as a vast library that you can bring into your home. A library full of information on any topic you can think of.

It is easy to say that the Internet is full of information. But how? Who puts it there?

All the information is held and displayed on Internet pages, called **web pages**. Information can be added and displayed by anyone, which means that companies, universities, shops and even individuals can make their own web page and present information on the Internet. Plus, nearly all of the information is freely available to anyone with a computer and a phone line, including you.

The Internet also allows you to communicate in new ways with family and friends, **email** being the most popular new communication tool. Email enables you to send written electronic messages to anyone, anywhere in the world, at the cost of a local telephone call.

Is the Internet dangerous?

As a vast library, the Internet is full of all sorts of information available at the click of a mouse. However, the Internet does not have strict censorship, so there is a need to exercise some individual censorship, especially if you are a parent with children who are also interested in exploring the Internet.

Another concern is that the Internet is full of computer hackers or con artists ready to rip you off. Have you ever come across a chain letter in the post or a prank telephone call? Well, the same sort of small-minded pranks and scams that happen in our daily lives have unfortunately crept on to the Internet. Although reported incidences are few and far between, it does mean that we should show the same caution on the Internet as we would normally show in daily activities.

Will the Internet take over everything we do?

Some people, who hear all the news stories and hype surrounding the Internet, become worried that it will take over everything they do.

While it is true that the Internet covers almost every topic, activity or business that you can think of, it is not here to replace things, just to make things easier and more accessible. Remember the Internet is all sorts of people, from all around the world, sharing ideas and information with each other. So it is bound to cover every topic imaginable!

Can you explain Internet jargon?

The normal rule of thumb is that when something new is invented, so too is a collection of words and sayings that form a new and confusing language. The Internet is no exception. Because jargon can be a real turn-off, this book has avoided as much of the new Internet language as possible. Nevertheless, you are bound to come across some, so here is an explanation of some of the most common Internet jargon.

The Internet is also referred to as the **world wide web** or just **the web**. Some people shorten the word Internet and just call it the **net**. For simplicity, this book will keep using the word **Internet**.

All the information that appears on the Internet appears on **web pages**. Web pages will contain written words, full-colour pictures, photographs, sounds and even movies. More than one connected web page will make up a **website**.

Even the act of using the Internet has its own jargon name. Using the Internet is referred to as **surfing** or **browsing**.

What are Internet Service Providers?

You need a telephone company to help you get a phone line or mobile phone or a cable television company if you decide to change to cable television. In the same way, to get a connection to the Internet for your computer you need help from an Internet Service Provider.

An Internet Service Provider will give you the connection you require to enable your home computer to become a place to access the Internet. They also provide a lot of support either via their Internet website or the telephone. This support is really handy if you are just starting out with the Internet or if you experience technical difficulties.

It doesn't really matter which ISP you choose. The only difference between them is the price or special offer you get and how the Internet buttons and toolbar will look on your computer screen.

Where do I start on the Internet?

With the amount of information available and the number of websites to visit this is a good question!

You want to start directly on those websites that you find most interesting. This book will show you how to get to these websites with the least amount of hassle and confusion. Turn a few pages and you'll soon be confident and inspired to jump to a starting place relevant to you.

Alternatively, you could begin with the **Home Internet Channel** website. I started this website when writing the book. For many, the vast number of

Internet websites can be daunting; even a single website can have too many buttons and links. So I designed this website as an easy and inspirational starting point for all your Internet adventures.

Find it at the website address **www.homeinternetchannel.com.**

What should I expect from the Internet?

Here is my list of what to expect from the Internet:

■ Expect a *never-ending* electronic magazine, full of information on just about anything and with stories and topics from around the world.

■ Also understand that this information can come from a professional company or professional source or it could just as easily be the opinion of the average person in the street.

■ Expect some minor technical difficulties. The Internet is not a perfect system. Sometimes a web page will take time to appear on your screen, sometimes you will get an error message that you don't understand. This book will explain how to overcome these faults.

■ Expect soon to have your favourite areas of the Internet. These will be the websites you will keep returning to when you are on the Internet.

■ Expect to start checking your email inbox daily for messages from family and friends once you realise how easy it is to keep in touch with email.

So now read on, to discover the Internet.

2
Easy Guide
to Internet Basics

The web page

The Internet is made up of millions of web pages. These are the pages that contain all the information, fun and excitement that attracts us to the Internet. All web pages look different on your computer screen: expect to see different colours, words, formats and advertising banners on each web page.

Overleaf is a typical web page as you see it on your screen. In fact, what you are actually looking at is a bit more than a web page. I'll explain.

The border around the web page, called the web browser, will always stay on your computer screen when you move from one web page to another. All these buttons and menus will help you visit web pages, print them, save them or leave them to go to another web page.

Inside this border is the web page itself – the main attraction and what we have come to see. This is the part of the screen that will change as you move around the Internet.

There are lots of web pages on the Internet. All of them look different and contain different information. Some will have a title at the top, like the headline on a newspaper. Below the title will be all the text and images which make up the information on the web page.

Your computer's scroll bar, in case the whole web page is too large to fit on the screen.

❶ This is the **web browser** – it contains all the tools that will help you get around the Internet and back and forth from web page to web page. This part of the web page never changes as you move between web pages.

❷ This white bar is the **address bar**. It is where you enter in a web page destination; hit Return, and you are taken to the web page.

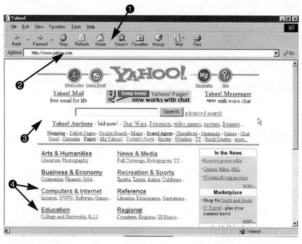

❸ This is the **web page** that you are visiting. The best way to describe a web page is that it is similar to page in a printed newspaper or magazine.

❹ Clicking on certain words and phrases that appear on the screen has the ability to take you to other pages within that website. Choosing one of these connections is like turning to a new page of a magazine.

What sites can you look at?

You can look at nearly any web page on the Internet. Many people worry that they will be charged for looking at website, especially the ones that undertake a service for you. No additional charge is made for visiting the majority of web pages and these can be accessed by anyone, anywhere in the world.

I say majority, because there are some *premium* web pages that do ask for payment before you can view them. This will be made clear to you by the web page, and you will have to enter your credit card details before any charge can be applied. So there is no need to worry about being unknowingly charged for visiting a web page.

Websites and web pages

Confused about the difference between a website and a web page?

In short, many web pages make up a website. Because a web page can only hold one page of information, the owner of the website will link together more than one web page to hold all the information and images.

Our job as Internet users is to look back and forth among the pages on a website to find all the information that interests us.

The web-page address

To find a web page we need to know the address of the web page. This **web address** is like a code. It is this code that tells your computer where to go and look for the web page on the Internet.

Also note that each web page has its own unique web address. Below are some examples of what a web address looks like.

➡ **http://www.homeinternetchannel.com**

➡ **http://www.yahoo.com**

➡ **http://www.altavista.com**

Breaking up the parts of a web address to explain what each part means, we get:

http://   www.   homeinternetchannel   .com

① **http://** – an Internet dialling code, like the area code in a phone number.
② **www.** – 'world wide web' abbreviated.
③ **homeinternetchannel** – the name of the website.
④ **.com** – the most common ending to a web address. Some others include:
   – **.gov** – signifies that it is a government site (**www.dti.gov**).
   – **.co.uk** – means that this website is UK based (**www.searchUK.co.uk**).
   – **.com.au** – indicates that the site is Australia based (**www.ozemail.com.au**).

Important things to know about web addresses:

① You must copy or type them correctly. Just like dialling a phone number, if you get one small thing incorrect, you will reach the wrong destination.

② Web addresses tend not to have spaces between the characters.

③ At first they look complicated, but after a while they will become second nature to anyone who uses the Internet.

Someone might tell you to look at a particular website and give you the address **www.homeinternetchannel.com** .They have omitted the **http://** at the beginning of the address because this is generic for every web address – it doesn't have to be repeated each time.

Visiting a website

Now that we understand what a web address is, let's try using one to locate a website on the Internet.

The web address bar

Inside your browser button panel, towards the top of your web page, there is a white box. This is the **web address box** or **web address bar**.

Whenever you visit a web page, the address of the page will be shown in this box. You can also use the address box to direct your computer to a web page that you want to visit. Here is how:

① Move the computer's cursor into the address box and type in the web address. You will have to delete the address that is currently in the address box before you start typing in the new one. In this case I want to visit the

❶ *The web address box or web address bar.*

Home Internet Channel web page, so I type **www.homeinter netchannel.com** within the box.

Most web browsers don't require you to add **http://** before the web address. With older web browsers, however, you may need to include this as well.
② Press Return on your keyboard or click **Go.**
③ In a few moments the web page that you wanted will appear on your computer.

What if the web page didn't appear?

If you didn't get through to the web page that you wanted and an **error message** appears, this could be for a number of reasons.
Check: that you correctly typed in the address. It must be 100% accurate or you will not find the web page that you want.
Check: you may have needed to add **http://** before the web address

A typical error message that appears when you have difficulty connecting to a web page.

If you still have problems, it may be because the computer system to that particular website is busy. The busy signal error message states: *'The connection is refused by the host'*. Don't worry, you haven't broken anything. If you try again in a few minutes you'll probably be successful.

What is a Home page?

The **Home page** is a special web page. Special because it is generally the first page of any website. Think of the Home page as being like the table of contents at the front of a book or magazine which helps you to locate where the different pages are inside.

Typing in a web address will always bring you to the website's Home page. The Home page will give you directions for visiting the rest of the website. Click on these directions to explore the website.

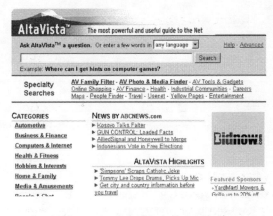

A typical Home page. Notice it looks like a table of contents in a magazine.

How to move around the Internet

You need to be able to move around the Internet and back and forth between web pages. So what you need is something like a TV remote control for the Internet.

When you connect to the web, you always have a 'remote control' around

While the buttons on your web browser may look different, they all do the same job.

the border of your web page. This is called a **web browser** and it lets you view what is on the Internet. If you have an Internet connection you will automatically have a browser on your computer.

Browsers have many features and uses. However, don't be daunted by this. In a few minutes you can learn the basics and start using the Internet. Then, in your own time, you can learn the more advanced functions of your browser.

Just as TV remote controls differ one from another and have different buttons, so too do web browsers. Here are two examples:

Don't worry if your browser doesn't look exactly like either of these. If you are connected through an **Internet Service Provider** (America Online, Compuserve, etc.) they will generally design their web browser to look different from others. They all do the same job.

It only takes a little practice and you'll soon be confident with the buttons on your particular web browser.

Web browser buttons

The row of buttons is called the **toolbar**. This is because it gives you the *tools* you need to look around the Internet.

The good news is that you don't need to know every single button on the tool bar to get started. I will describe the ones you should know to get going, then I suggest you try them! We will come to the rest later on.

Back button
Clicking on the **Back** button returns you to the web page you were previously on. It is like turning back a page in a book. Click the button twice and you will move back two pages.

Forward button
If you have used the Back button to go back a web page, use the **Forward** button to return to where you were originally. You need to have used the Back button before you can use the Forward button.

Home button
The **Home** button always takes you back to the Home page or start page. This will be the first start page that appears on your screen each time you connect to the Internet.

Reload or Refresh button
Sometimes when you try to visit a web page there might be a problem with your computer making the electronic connection to that web page. This will result in not all of the web page loading properly. The **Reload** button will try the connection again and refresh the half-opened web page.

Stop button
The **Stop** button stops your web browser from searching for the current web page. This is a really handy button if the web pages are taking a really

long time to appear on your computer screen and you want to quit and try something else.

 Print button
If you have a printer, it is great to be able to print out any information, recipes, stories or advice that you have found on the Internet. The **Print** button will send the web page that you are currently viewing to the printer for you.

Get going NOW! You don't need any more knowledge to start having fun on the Internet. Start up your computer, select the Internet option and, beginning with the web page that automatically appears on your screen, start moving from web page to web page. Don't forget to use the handy little tools on the previous page to help you move back and forth between the pages you visit.

Quick links

You'll notice that on a web page there is always text in a different colour or some-times underlined, e.g. <u>See next page</u>. These underlined words appear in the main written paragraphs or sometimes they will appear in a list, like the contents page in a book. As you move the cursor over these links, the cursor arrow will change to a small hand. What does this mean?

It means that there is an automatic **link** to another web page. Clicking your left mouse button on a link will move you from your current web page to a new one. For example:

Clicking on the word <u>News</u> will take you to the news web page. Likewise moving the cursor down to the <u>Sports</u> section will move you to the sports web page. It is simply turning a web page electronically to go to another one.

Try it. Visit any web page, then move your cursor � around the screen and watch it change into a hand ✋. When you find something that looks interesting, click on that word or phrase and wait for the new web page to appear on your screen.

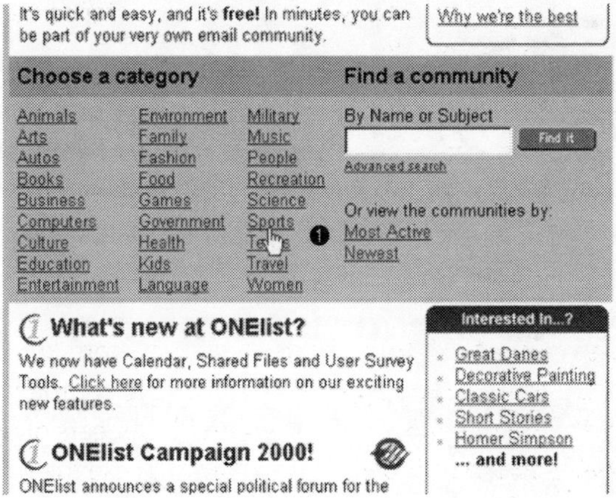

It's quick and easy, and it's **free!** In minutes, you can be part of your very own email community. | <u>Why we're the best</u>

Choose a category

<u>Animals</u>	<u>Environment</u>	<u>Military</u>
<u>Arts</u>	<u>Family</u>	<u>Music</u>
<u>Autos</u>	<u>Fashion</u>	<u>People</u>
<u>Books</u>	<u>Food</u>	<u>Recreation</u>
<u>Business</u>	<u>Games</u>	<u>Science</u>
<u>Computers</u>	<u>Government</u>	<u>Sports</u>
<u>Culture</u>	<u>Health</u>	<u>Te..</u>
<u>Education</u>	<u>Kids</u>	<u>Travel</u>
<u>Entertainment</u>	<u>Language</u>	<u>Women</u>

Find a community

By Name or Subject
[ ] [Find it]
<u>Advanced search</u>

Or view the communities by:
<u>Most Active</u>
<u>Newest</u>

What's new at ONElist?

We now have Calendar, Shared Files and User Survey Tools. <u>Click here</u> for more information on our exciting new features.

ONElist Campaign 2000!

ONElist announces a special political forum for the

Interested In...?

· <u>Great Danes</u>
· <u>Decorative Painting</u>
· <u>Classic Cars</u>
· <u>Short Stories</u>
· <u>Homer Simpson</u>
  ... and more!

❶ *Examples of links on a web page.*

Sports
T... e

/e now have Calendar
ools. <u>Click here</u> for m(
ew feature

Notice the computer's arrow cursor changes to a small hand.

3
Easy Guide
to Finding Things on the Internet

Searching for information

We know there is lots of fun and interesting information on the web. Now we need to know how to get at it. The easiest way to get information on the web is to get someone else to do the hard work!

There are services on the Internet that will help you to find the information you want. These services are called **search engines** and are an easy place for beginners to start. Imagine a search engine as a telephone directory. But *this* telephone directory does the

➡ www.yahoo.com

looking for you and tells you what page your information is on.

You need first to tell the search engine what to look for. It then goes out and searches the whole Web for you and brings back all the websites that match what you are looking for. The great thing about a search engine is that it organises and often ranks the websites that it found for you, making your job a whole lot easier.

Where can you find a search engine?

Search engines look like any normal web page on the Internet.

➡ **www.altavista.com**

➡ **www.looksmart.com**

3 typical search engines (this page and opposite)

Just like any other website, they have their own special web address (e.g. **http:// www. search-engine.com**). This leads directly to the search engine's **Home page** where we start our search for information.

Reminder! – A Home page is the very first page of any website. It's a bit like a table of contents in a book.

Search engines

All search engines look different on your computer screen. The good news is that all search engines work in basically the same way. Learn to use one, and you will be able to use them all.

Generally a search engine will look like the one opposite. Don't worry about all the other stuff on the page; at this stage, all we need to get going is the **search box** (1).

Now let's go and find some information on your favourite hobby on the web.

Step-by-step guide to searching

– Switch on your computer and connect to the Internet.
– When your web browser is ready, go to the **address box** and type in **http://www.altavista.com** . **Altavista** is one of the web's biggest search engines as well as being an easy one to use.

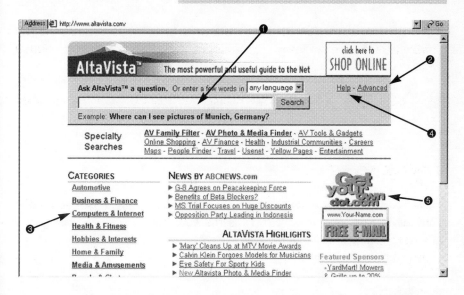

① This blank white box is the search box. It is where you type in what you want to look for. The search box is normally found at the top of the search engine web page.

② **Advanced options and preferences:** search engines are designed to help you find what you want quickly. They give you these tools to make your search more specific. We'll cover this later.

③ **Popular sites and categories:** these make it easier for you to search by listing broad categories and subjects which you may be interested in.

④ **Help** or **FAQs** (frequently asked questions): all web engines offer help in using their service. Generally these instructions are very easy to understand, so just click the button and read away.

⑤ **Advertising:** advertisers pay the search engines to put up a billboard on their website. This electronic bill-board generally appears as a long box called a **banner**.

– After you have typed in the address, click the **Go** button and the Home page of Altavista will appear on your screen. Now Altavista is ready to search for any information on the web you want.

– Find the Altavista search box (hint – that's the blank white box near the top of the screen).

AltaVista™ The most powerful and useful guide to the Net

Ask AltaVista™ a question. Or enter a few words in [any language ▼]   Help - Advanced

[❶   ] [Search]

Example: **Where can I find the web site for Levis?**

❶ *The search box*

– When you have found it, type your favourite hobby into this box, e.g. if you like gardening, type in '*gardening*'. The word 'gardening' becomes a **keyword** for your search. You should type your keyword in lower case letters unless you know that the keyword should begin with a capital letter. Now press the Search button.

AltaVista™ The most powerful and useful guide to the Net

Ask AltaVista™ a question. Or enter a few words in [any language ▼]   Help - Advanced

[Gardening   ] [Search]

Example: **Where can I find the web site for Levis?**

Enter the search word in this space.
Then press Search.

– Wait a few moments while Altavista is searching the web.

– A list of different 'websites' will soon appear on the Altavista Home page.

✓ Congratulations! You have just used a search engine to find something for you!

Understanding the results of your search

The search engine has just done a lot of work for you.

You told it to go out on to the world wide web and search for all the websites that had something to do with your hobby. What the search engine actually did was go look for all the websites that had the keyword you typed in (i.e. *gardening*) included somewhere in the information on that website.

➤ **AltaVista found 492170 Web pages for you.**

gardening - List of near matches related to **gardening** provided by RealNames.

1. **Reeds 'n Weeds Water Gardening Superstore | fax/mail order form**
   return to the reeds 'n weeds store. PRINT THIS PAGE FOR A FAX or MAIL-IN ORDER FORM. FAX TO (606) 887-5775 24 hours a day, 7 days a week. Orders only. OR.
   URL: www.reedsnweeds.com/orderform.htm
   Last modified 31-Mar-99 · page size 7K · in English [Translate]

2. **Traditional Gardening: Main Menu**
   URL: traditionalgardening.com/
   Last modified 15-Apr-99 · page size 6K · in English [Translate]

3. **Gardening: Garden Gate Magazine Online**
   Garden Gate Magazine -- The Illustrated Guide to Home Gardening and ..
   URL: www.augusthome.com/gardeng.htm
   Last modified 22-Mar-99 · page size 5K · in English [Translate]

4. **Gardening Books from Timber Press**
   Gardening Books from Timber Press...

Books at Amazon.com
Search: Gardening
Save up to 50%

AltaVista Shopping
Visit our Online
Shopping Guide

Shop at Shopping.com
Search: Gardening
Daily specials below cost

Results are presented to you in a list.

The search engine will tell you how many websites it found that matched your keyword and could be of interest to you. One keyword will bring up thousands of useful websites but it will probably also bring up thousands of useless ones too.

Don't panic if it tells you it has found over a million websites for you to look at! That is quite normal. Remember that the web contains tonnes of information from all around the world. So you could easily be directed to the website of someone living in Canada who shares your hobby!

Each website that is found can be called a **result** or a **hit**. The result will look something like this:

❶   *WEB PAGE NAME*
❷   *A brief description of what*
    information this website
    contains about your hobby.
    What other information it
    has that is relevant to your
    hobby. What categories are
    included in the website.
❸   *The web address*
❹   *Information about the*
    website and when it was
    updated.

On the same page, the search engine will list all the websites it has found for you. If there are many results, or hits, you may find there will be more than one page for you to look at and select from. The search engine will make it possible for you to move back and forth between the pages of these results. Look for the **Next page** or a **Get Next Results** buttons towards the bottom of the web page. These buttons will let you browse through the results one page at a time.

After reviewing the list of results, use your mouse to pick a website that you

❶ *Search engines will*
make it easy for you to see
all the results.

URL: www.familygardening.com/page2.html
Last modified 21-Mar-99 - page size 17K - in English [Translate]

10. Get Connected...Garden Centre, Gardening Internet Resource. Information, tips,
    Garden Centre offers tips, information pages and help for gardeners. This is index page 1 offers
    links to gardening...
    URL: www.familygardening.com/connect.html
    Last modified 20-Mar-99 - page size 27K - in English [Translate]

Result Pages: 1 2 3 4 5 6 7 8 9 10 11 12 13 14 15 16 17 18 19 20 [**Next >>**]
word count: Gardening: 229093

are interested in visiting. The arrow cursor will change to a small hand which means it is a link

10. Get Connected...Garden Centre. Gardening Internet Resource. Information. tips.
  Garden Centre offers tips, information pages and help for gardeners. This is index page 1
  links to gardening...
  URL: www.familygardening.com/connect.html
  Last modified 20-Mar-99 - page size 27K - in English [Translate]

to another site. Simply click your left mouse button and your computer will be told to go and visit the website that you have chosen.

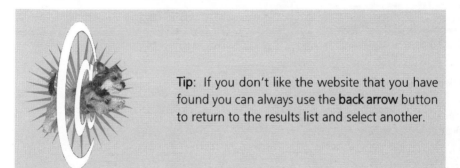

Tip: If you don't like the website that you have found you can always use the **back arrow** button to return to the results list and select another.

Other search engines

In the step-by-step guide above, we used the search engine Altavista to find websites that matched your hobby. Altavista is not the only search engine to use on the web – there are plenty of others to choose from.

You may have found that your search included too many foreign websites in the results. While some of these may be interesting, you may want to look specifically for sites in the UK or Australia. There are specialist search engines which make this possible and should return results which are more useful to you.

Always look towards the bottom of your favourite search engine's Home page to see if it offers a special search engine for your country.

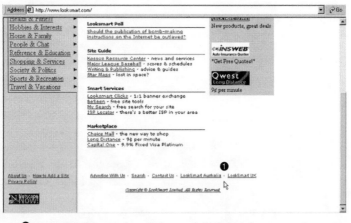

❶ *Look to see if the search engine has a website dedicated to your country.*

On the opposite page is a list of some of the best search engines and their web addresses for you to try.

Many people wonder which search engine they should use for the best results. There is no right answer to this. They all do the same job of searching the web for you, but the results that you get can vary from one search engine to another. This is not a problem; it just means that you will get different results according to which search engine you use.

Some people like using more than one search engine at a time. This allows them to compare the results with those of other search engines.

So I would encourage you to try several search engines from the ones listed below. Why not ask your friends which ones they like to use? Soon you will have found the search engine that you feel most comfortable with and will use it regularly for your web searches.

Remember that there is no limit to what you can search for – so happy searching!

Name	Web Address
Altavista	➡ **www.altavista.com**
Yahoo	➡ **www.yahoo.com**
	➡ **www.yahoo.co.uk**
	➡ **www.yahoo.com.au**

LookSmart   ➡ **www.looksmart.com**
                 ➡ **www.looksmart.co.uk**
                 ➡ **www.looksmart.com.au**

Excite   ➡ **www.excite.com**

SearchUK   ➡ **www.searchuk.com**

UKPlus   ➡ **www.ukplus.co.uk**

Britannica Internet Guide   ➡ **www.ebig.com** (great for kids' projects!)

4
Easy Guide
to Email

What is email?

Email is the Internet's electronic postal system. A message can be sent from your computer to any other computer in the world – and no stamp is required. With email you have the opportunity to receive greetings or news from family and friends directly via your own email mailbox.

The idea of sending a message from one computer to another may seem to be more trouble than it is worth initially. However, once you have grasped the concept of email and start sending and receiving these electronic messages, you will end up using your email every day.

Why use email?

Email is probably the most popular tool available on the Internet so don't be surprised if it becomes your favourite. Here are some of the many reasons why email is so popular:

■ Messages can be sent to *anyone* with an email address *anywhere* in the world *instantaneously*. This means that a friend or relative in the USA doesn't have to wait a week for your letter to arrive by post. Plus, on receiving your email, they can send you an immediate reply.

■ You can receive email even when your computer is switched off. The messages sent to you will be stored in your mailbox until you connect to your email program again. This also means that you can send an email to someone without having to worry about an engaged phone line or people not being at home to receive it. Your message will be waiting for them when they next check their mailbox.

■ The same email can be sent to many friends at the same time. This is very handy for party invitations!

■ It doesn't matter where you send an email or how long it is, it will only ever cost you the price of a local phone call to connect your computer to the Internet. There are no long-distance charges on the Internet. For example, if you want to send out invitations to ten friends, you can do so with one email message within five minutes – compare this to the price of ten stamps or the cost of ten telephone calls.

Email basics explained

Sending an email is simple once you grasp the basics. All it involves is typing a message, choosing who you will send it to, and clicking the Send button.

There are lots of special things that you can do with email. But first let's concentrate on the basics of sending a message to someone. Below is the list of things you will need to get started. You will already have a connection to the Internet, but the email program and the email address need some explanation.

What you need:
    ① *connection to the Internet*
    ② *email program*
    ③ *the email address of a friend or relative*

The email program

The **email program** helps you send, receive and organise your emails. It is like having your own private post office on your home computer. The email program will give you everything you need for your 'computer post office'. This will include being able to send emails, to keep an address

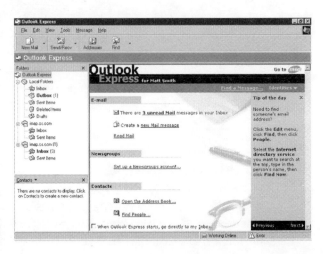

Example of a typical email program.

book, and to visit your mailbox to collect incoming messages. Your email mailbox or **inbox** is where you can collect emails that have been sent to you.

Where do you get an email program?

If you connect to the Internet with an Internet Service Provider, they will provide you with an email service. They should also be able to supply you with instructions on how to use their email program.

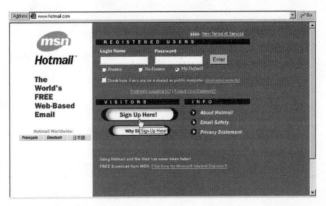

The totally free Hotmail email website.

Or you might choose to use the email program that comes with your Internet browser. For the Explorer browser the email program is called **Outlook Express**. For the Netscape browser it is called **Messenger.**

A final option is to use a website email program, straight from the Internet. These email websites are a one-stop shop which provides everything you need to send and receive emails. A good example for a website email account is **Hotmail** found at web address **www.hotmail.com** .

Whatever program you have or use, the basics are the same. The only difference is in how they look.

The email address

An **email address** works in the same way as a street address. Your email address is effectively the address of your Internet postbox. So just as the post office uses your street name and number to send you post, the Internet uses your email address to send you your emails.

There is, however, an important difference when sending an email instead of a letter. Unlike regular post, the email address must be absolutely correct. Near enough won't be good enough. A spelling or punctuation error when typing an email address will mean that your message will not be sent to where you want it to go. So you must make sure, when entering the email addresses of your family or friends, that you write them correctly – down to the last dot!

Everyone finds email addresses rather strange at first so don't worry if you feel the same – you will soon be using them as easily as postal addresses. An email address looks like this:

matt.smith	**@**	**homeinternetchannel**	**.com**
My name	At	Where I am	the common address ending

So all email addresses can be read as: *someone 'at' a place on the Internet*. Sometimes people use nicknames or initials in their email address. It doesn't even have to be their real name.

The third part of the address – where the person is – is the place that handles and organises their emails. Generally it will be one of two locations. It will be the person's place of work or, if it is a home email account, it will be their email provider, e.g. AOL, Freeserve, Hotmail etc.

Note: Remember I said you have to be accurate when writing emails? Well, if you tried to contact me at either of the email addresses below, neither would get through to me. Accuracy is essential!

m.smith@homeinternetchannel.com

or

matt<space>smith@homeinternetchannel.com

What is your email address?

If you are signed up to an Internet Service Provider then you should automatically have an email address. If you don't know what it is, ask your Internet provider to explain it to you.

If you set up a Hotmail account, your email address will be allocated to you during the signing-up process.

Tip: A Hotmail account is really handy if you have an email address at work but would like to have an additional one for personal and private use. Or maybe another member of the family would like to have an email address of their own.

Whatever the reason, Hotmail accounts are free, so why not have a go?

Sending an email

Your first step is to enter the **email area** or **email centre** on your computer.

If you are using the email program supplied by your Internet Service Provider or attached to your browser, start the email program via the **File** menu or the **Send Email** button on your browser.

If you are using a website email service, like Hotmail, you

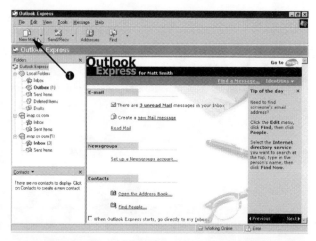

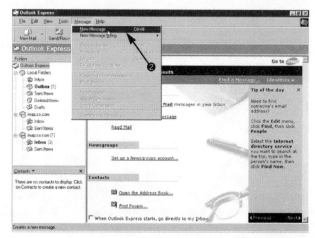

Either ❶ click on the New Mail button or ❷ choose the New Message option from the message menu.
The blank New Message email box will appear on your computer screen.

need to visit the Hotmail website each time you want to use email.

① Select the **New Message** or **Create Mail** option. A window should then appear which looks something like a blank postcard. This is where you write your message and enter an email address.

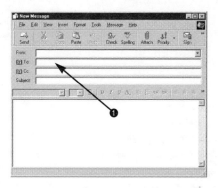

② Enter your intended recipient's **email address** into the address box. Either ask a friend or relative for their email address, as a test, or you could try sending an email to yourself, by entering your own email address in the address box.

❶ *Enter the recipient's email address in the blank address box.*

③ Although it is not always necessary, it is useful for the recipient if you type in the **subject** of your email. If you want to tell the recipient about your weekend, the subject could be: 'My weekend'.

④ Type in your email message in the large blank area beneath the address box.

❷ *This is where you type in the subject of your email.*

⑤ When you have finished and are happy with what you have written, click the **Send** button or choose the **Send** option from the file menu.

You will get an onscreen confirmation that your email has been sent. Remember, you must be connected to the Internet for your email to be sent.

Clicking the **Send** button will post the email to your friend.

Tips for writing emails

A lot of people are unsure as to how they should write an email. What do you put in the subject line, how long should it be, how should you sign off the email message?

There are no set rules for writing emails. Messages can be as formal or as informal as you like. They can be as long or as short as you like. Below are some guidelines to help you in writing emails.

The subject line

Most often the subject line is used to summarise or introduce the major ideas contained in the message. You only get a limited space to write in the subject, so try to summarise it in a couple of words.

If you are just sending a quick greeting message, just type in the subject: HELLO!!

The greeting

When you write a letter you generally start with a greeting of some sort. Similar rules apply, depending on who you are addressing, when sending emails.

Dear Matt – a formal opening which a lot of beginners prefer to use.

Hello Matt or **Hi Matt** – a more casual opening which is generally preferred because email is viewed as a more casual form of communication than letter-writing.

The body of the message

This is entirely up to you. You can write in paragraphs, with or without bullet points, or it could be just a single sentence or a question.

The sign-off

Because you can't sign your message by hand, most people like to add some sort of typed sign-off at the end of their email, such as *Regards* or *Take care*, by way of conclusion.

You might also want to include your email address under your name in case the recipient does not have it.

Reading email messages

Any messages that are sent to you are collected by your email mailbox or **inbox**. It acts just like any normal post office box or letterbox. The emails will wait in your inbox until you collect them.

The two ways you can get to your email inbox.

To open your inbox and check for any email, you click on the **Received Message** button or **Unread mail** button on your email start page.

A list of the messages that you have received will appear in a summary list, with brief details about each message.

Each email contains the date on which it was sent, the sender's name, and the subject of the message.

To read a message, choose the one you want, then either double click on it directly with your

❶ *The list of email messages that have been sent to the inbox.*

mouse or select it and click the **Read Mail** button. The email message will appear on your computer screen with ❶ the details of who sent it, ❷ when it was sent and ❸ the message itself.

Closing or deleting an email message

After you have read or replied to a message, you can close the email by closing the window in which the message appears. The email that you were reading will disappear off your computer screen but it will still be in your inbox to read again should you want to.

Alternatively, if you don't think you will want to read the message again, click on the **Delete** button and the email will be removed altogether from your inbox. The Delete email function is especially useful when your mailbox starts overflowing with messages. To keep things organised you'll want to remove emails that you no longer need, rather than have them clutter your inbox.

❶ *Who sent the email*
❷ *When it was sent*
❸ *The message.*

Clicking the Delete Message will delete any trace of the email you have just read. Alternatively, just close the email if you think you may want to read it again.

5
Getting the Most
from Your Web Browser

In the 'Easy Guide to Internet Basics' we looked at the following tools on the **web browser**:

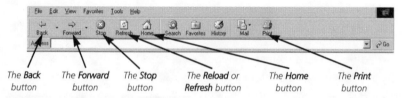

The **Back**   The **Forward**   The **Stop**   The **Reload** or   The **Home**   The **Print**
button   button   button   **Refresh** button   button   button

In addition to these basic controls that help you to navigate back and forth between web pages, your browser has other features that will enable you to travel around the Internet even more quickly and easily. Again, take your time learning these features. Pick one at a time. Try it, experiment with it and see if you think you will find it useful. You don't have to know every button and feature on your web browser in order to enjoy the Internet.

The hints and tips in this chapter include:

■ The drop-down box
■ The History menu
■ Bookmarking favourite web pages

■ Speeding up your Internet
■ Personalising your Internet

The drop-down box

Inside your browser button panel, towards the top of your web page, there is the **web address box** or **web address bar**. Whenever you visit a web page, its address will be shown in this box.

You will also notice that there is a small downward-pointing arrow to the right of the web address box.

Notice the small downward-pointing arrow at the side of your address box.

Clicking on this arrow will reveal a **drop-down box** which contains a list of website addresses. Looking closely, you will see that these addresses are the

websites that you have been viewing recently, arranged in the order that you visited them. Each time you move to a new web page, this list will get longer. You can use the drop-down box as a handy

❶ *Position the cursor over the web address you want to select, then double-click with your mouse button – the website will appear in a few moments.*

way of jumping back to a recently visited web page without having to type in the web page address again or using the back arrow button.

All you do is get the drop-down window to appear on your computer screen, select the website that you want to go to with the cursor and, with the mouse, double-click on the website address. The website will appear on your screen in a few seconds.

The History menu
As you jump from web page to web page, your web browser remembers and records where you have been. This information is recorded in your **History folder**. The History folder records all the websites that you have visited recently.

To see the websites that you have previously been visiting, access your history folder by clicking on the **History** button on your browser toolbar.

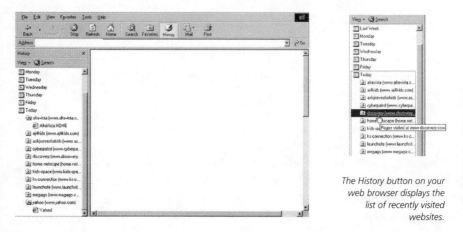

The History button on your web browser displays the list of recently visited websites.

The list is organised in order of the time when the websites were visited. Not only is it a useful reminder of the websites you have been visiting, but a double mouse click on any of the displayed web addresses will take you back to that web page.

Note that the list of web pages in the History menu is refreshed after a period of time. How often this happens will depend on your web browser. So if you really like a website you should save it as a **Bookmark** or **Favourite** site, rather than relying on it being in the History menu.

Bookmarking favourite web pages

The most basic way to access a website is to enter the website's address into the browser address box. This must be typed in 100% accurately for your web browser to find the site that you want.

As you use the Internet more and more, you will probably come across web pages that you find particularly interesting or useful and you'll end up visiting them every time you use the Internet. If you visit a site regularly, it can become quite a chore to type in the web address each time, let alone remember it. Thankfully, you can make your web browser remember the address for you.

To do so, you tell your web browser to create a bookmark on the web page. They are called bookmarks because they are 'electronic dog ears' marking a favourite place on the Internet.

Bookmarks are sometimes referred to as Favourites. This will depend on your web browser or the Internet Service Provider you subscribe to.

Bookmarks or Favourites save the addresses of your favourite sites in a list. This list is easily accessed by you at any time you want. There will be no need to type in a web address all over again; just visit your Bookmark or Favourite list and select your website automatically from there.

Creating a bookmark

① Visit the web page that you want to bookmark. Stay on that web page.

② Next, look for the **Favourite** or **Bookmark** button or option on your web browser. Select the **Add Favourite** or **Add Bookmark** option from the menu that appears on your screen.

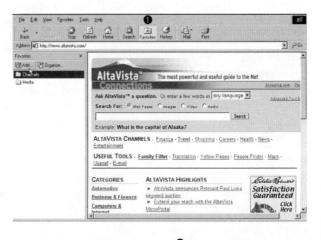

❶ *Having located the Favourite or Bookmark area, select the ADD option* ❷. *This will add the current website you are on to the bookmark list.*

You have now told your browser to remember the current web page as being a favourite of yours. When you return to the Bookmark or Favourite section, the web page that you bookmarked will be on the list. It will stay on this list even after you switch off your computer.

Using bookmarks or favourites

To look up a website you have previously bookmarked, select the Bookmark or Favourite button or option on your web browser.

Your list of favourites will appear in a menu format. Simply double mouse click on the particular favourite you want to revisit and it will automatically appear on your screen.

Use the bookmark list like an address book. Look up your favourite sites and double mouse click on the one you want to go to. If you have bookmarked it, there is no more need to remember or type in a web address!

Organising bookmarks

You'll soon find that your bookmark address book will be overrun and disorganised because you'll always be adding interesting sites that you want to return to – particularly if everyone at home is adding their favourites to the bookmark list and not just you!

Organising this potential overflow of bookmarks is easy, but it will take a little time to decide how you are going to categorise your favourite websites.

Within your bookmark or favourites area, you will find that you have the option to **Organise Favourites.**

The Organise feature allows you to create electronic folders in which to store your bookmarks. An electronic folder works in exactly the same way as a real folder on a bookshelf. After choosing the **Create File** option, you need to name the newly created

The Organise Favourites appears in the book-mark or favourite area.

Create a new folder to keep similar book-marks inside. If they are search engine websites, then call the folder Favourite Search Engines for easy reference.

Move your search engine bookmarks into the Search Engine folder.

file. For search engine websites, for example, call the folder *Search Engines*; for news websites, call it *News*.

Once this folder has been created, you can move any related bookmarks into it, using the **Move to Folder** option. Select the website you want to move to a particular folder. In this case it is the Altavista bookmark. Having selected the website, click on the Move to Folder button.

Just repeat the steps above to create more folders and organise the rest of your bookmarks. Within a few minutes you'll have a well-organised bookmark or favourites section.

Bookmark Do's and Don'ts

Do spend time learning how your bookmark or favourites area works. It won't take long to master how to use it – and you'll thank yourself that you did.

Do ring your Internet Service Provider technical support if you are having difficulties.

Don't forget to add a bookmark whenever you discover a great new web page. Nothing is as frustrating as forgetting where it was when you want to return to it the following day.

Don't let your bookmark or favourites section get out of control. Keeping it organised in folders will make things easier and quicker to find, especially if more than one person at home is adding their favourites to a growing list.

Do delete any bookmarks that are no longer required, rather than letting them add to the clutter.

Do ask your friends which websites they bookmark. This is a good way of adding to the range of interesting sites you visit.

Do search the Internet for more bookmarking tips and hints.

Speeding up the Internet

The Stop button

The **Stop** button can be really useful in speeding up your use of the Internet.

When you visit a web page, the text will always appear on the screen first and the pictures and images will take longer to materialise. Sometimes you can wait quite a long time for an image to appear.

If you are only interested in the text on a website, press the Stop button once this has appeared rather than waiting for a slow image or picture to follow. Your computer will stop loading the web page before the pictures appear. This will allow you to read the text on the web page without waiting around for the pictures to come up on your screen.

❶ *Use the Stop button to stop your browser loading the web page.*

If you want to see the image later, click the **Refresh** or **Reload** button to continue loading a web page.

Visiting two websites at once

It is handy to know how to view two web pages simultaneously on your screen.

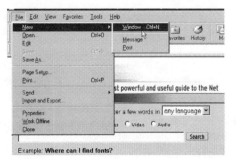

Most browsers will let you open a second web page via the File menu. This will allow you to run two web pages simultaneously.

For example, if it is taking time for something to appear or load on a web page, it would be good to have a favourite news website open to read while you are waiting.

To do this, go to the menu bar at the very top of your computer screen and select the File menu. Then select the option **New:** this will either be the option **New Web Browser** or **New Window**.

This will create a second screen on which to open a new web page. With some smart manoeuvring and adjusting of the two web pages you should be able to see both at the same time.

Warning! While it is clever and useful, having two web pages open simultaneously does slow down your computer. So if you are finding things too slow, stick to the single web page.

Personalising your Internet

This is a very useful tip which, however simple, will really make you feel like an Internet pro! It will also ensure that you don't waste time getting to your favourite and most visited websites.

When you normally turn on your computer, you will first arrive at your desktop screen page.

Your desktop opening screen page with the various icons.

On your desktop screen page you will see a row of handy little icons. With one click on these icons your word processor or your spreadsheet programs will automatically start. These icons are called **shortcuts**. You will probably also have an icon to connect you quickly to the Internet.

If you have a favourite web page that you visit when you first connect to the Internet, then you can create a shortcut icon for that web page. When it has been created, clicking on this shortcut will not only start the Internet for you, it will also automatically take you to your favourite website.

How to create a shortcut

Reduce the size of your Internet screen so that you can see the desktop in the background. You can do this by clicking the button in the top-right-hand corner of your screen.

Open up your favourites or book-mark list. Select the bookmark that you want to make into a shortcut icon. In this

*Select the bookmark for which you want to create a shortcut icon.
Drag the selected bookmark by keeping your finger on the left mouse button.
Drop it on to your desktop by releasing the left mouse button.*

case the **www.homeinternetchannel.com** bookmark is selected.

Drag this bookmark across your screen and on to your desktop by holding down the left-hand mouse button. Only let go of the left mouse button when you want to drop the item.

Your web-page icon should now be created on your desktop page. So no more messing around with typing a web address repetitively for access to your favourite site. One click on your shortcut icon and you are there!

6
More on Searching
the Internet

Search engines are great because they make finding information on the Internet very easy. Everyone who uses the Internet will use search engines regularly, so it is a good idea to know how to use them to their full potential.

There are some very easy ways in which you can improve your searching techniques. Whatever search engine you prefer to use, the following hints and tips will help to improve your ability to search for the precise information you want.

Don't worry about learning all of them at once. Try to master them one at a time. You can always refer back to this page if you want to learn some more techniques to combine with the ones you already know.

Let's see how these tips can help us improve our search for websites with information on holidays in the USA.

Tips for improving a search

If your **search word** or **phrase** is too broad, you will be presented with thousands of websites. The more precise you can be with your search criteria, the fewer non-related websites you will have to trawl through in the results list.

Tip 1 – Use **quotation marks**

"Holidays in the USA"	**Search**

Putting a search phrase between quotation marks will mean that the search engine only selects web pages on which the quoted phrase appears, rather than the component words. For example, it will search the websites for 'Holidays in the USA' rather than for references just to 'Holidays' and 'USA'.

Tip 2 – Inserting '**AND**' or '**+**' between words

Holidays AND USA	**Search**

Inserting 'AND' or the addition sign '+' between search words will ensure that the search engine will select web pages on which *both* the word '*holiday*' and the word '*USA*' appear, though not necessarily together.

Note: 'AND' must be in capital letters; or, if using the '+' sign, there must not be a space between the sign and the word.

Tip 3 – Inserting '**AND NOT**' or '**–**' between words.

Holidays AND NOT skiing	**Search**

Inserting 'AND NOT' or the '–' 'minus' sign between search words will result in a list of websites that *don't* include a particular word. For example, if you wanted a 'Holidays' website but didn't want information on skiing, you could enter 'Holidays AND NOT skiing'.

<u>Tip 4</u> – Inserting '**OR**' between words

Holidays OR flights	Search

Inserting 'OR' between search words will give you a list of websites that contain both words, either separately or together. This is useful when you are finding that your results are becoming a little *too* narrow. For example, searching 'Holidays OR Flights' would give you websites not just on holidays or just on flights, but those that included both words.

Tip 5 – Remember **CAPITALS**

Holidays AND USA	Search

If your search word or phrase is capital sensitive, e.g., *USA*, *New York*, *Chrysler*, then make sure you always use capitals where required.

Tip 6 – Use an **asterisk***

travel*	Search

An asterisk* after a word will produce results that include not only your search word but also the word with all its different endings. If you wanted to look at travel sites, for example, a search entry *'travel*'* would give you results that included traveller, travelling, travels, travelled, etc.

Tip 7 – Title Only search

Title: Holiday	Search

If you think your search word might appear as part of the title of some websites, why not try a Title Only search? These can often produce useful results.

Tip 8 – Image Only search

Image: USA	Search

If you are only interested in finding sites with pictures or images of your topic, use the Image Only search which will specifically look for images which have titles containing your search word.

Understanding your results

Once you have used a search engine to search for a keyword or phrase, the next and more challenging part of the process is evaluating the list of results that you get from your search.

The number of results you obtain can run into hundreds of thousands. The relevance or usefulness can vary from one result to the next and you can easily become frustrated by this. However, with a little understanding of the results, this frustration can be minimised.

Results are presented in numerous ways. Some search engines list the results by title, some include a brief description of the site, and some even let you choose how the results are to be presented.

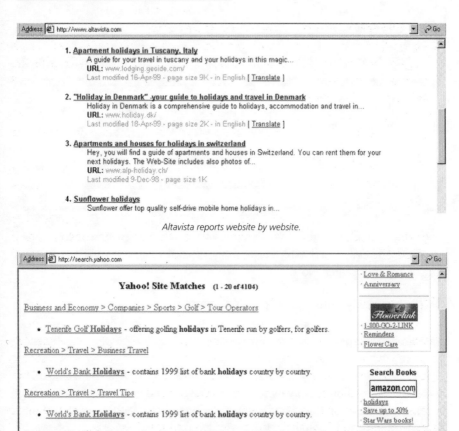

Address 🔁 http://www.altavista.com ▾ ⟳ Go

1. **Apartment holidays in Tuscany, Italy**
   A guide for your travel in tuscany and your holidays in this magic...
   URL: www.lodging.geoide.com/
   Last modified 16-Apr-99 - page size 9K - in English [Translate]

2. **"Holiday in Denmark" -your guide to holidays and travel in Denmark**
   Holiday in Denmark is a comprehensive guide to holidays, accommodation and travel in...
   URL: www.holiday.dk/
   Last modified 18-Apr-99 - page size 2K - in English [Translate]

3. **Apartments and houses for holidays in switzerland**
   Hey, you will find a guide of apartments and houses in Switzerland. You can rent them for your
   next holidays. The Web-Site includes also photos of...
   URL: www.alp-holiday.ch/
   Last modified 9-Dec-98 - page size 1K

4. **Sunflower holidays**
   Sunflower offer top quality self-drive mobile home holidays in...

Altavista reports website by website.

Address 🔁 http://search.yahoo.com ▾ ⟳ Go

· Love & Romance
· Anniversary

Yahoo! Site Matches (1 - 20 of 4104)

Business and Economy > Companies > Sports > Golf > Tour Operators

- Tenerife Golf Holidays - offering golfing **holidays** in Tenerife run by golfers, for golfers.

Recreation > Travel > Business Travel

- World's Bank Holidays - contains 1999 list of bank **holidays** country by country.

Recreation > Travel > Travel Tips

- World's Bank Holidays - contains 1999 list of bank **holidays** country by country.

Recreation > Travel > By Region > Countries > United Kingdom > England > Complete Listing

- Blackpool Holidays - lodging, attractions, events, and more.

Flowerlink
· 1-800-OO-2-LINK
· Reminders
· Flower Care

Search Books
amazon.com
holidays
· Save up to 50%
· Star Wars books!

Yahoo! reports results on a category basis.

What to look for with search-engine results:

① Generally it is wise to start with the top few ranked results because search engines will report on the most relevant first. If these results seem a far cry from what you were trying to find, you may want to check the search word you used or the spelling of the word.

② Although a brief description of the website will be included in the results list, you may still have to visit the website to get an understanding of what it contains.

③ If your search produces pages and pages of results, don't waste time trawling through all of them. You'll probably find what you are after in the first few pages.

④ If you want to retry your search, but you are stuck for another search word or phrase, you could find a better phrase or search word in the original list of results.

Trying other search engines

It is helpful to know that no search engine searches every website on the Internet. Knowing this fact, if your first search doesn't produce the results you wanted, try searching the same keyword with another search engine. A good idea is to have at least two favourite search engines which you feel comfortable using. It is always worth asking friends or family what search engines they use and what features they particularly like about their favourite search engines.

While this book cannot feature all the benefits of each particular search engine, the search engines themselves always have sections which will explain the ins and outs of their particular way of working. Although these may take a

All search engines will have handy Help sections like those of Yahoo! and Altavista.
These Help sections are accessed by clicking on the Help button.

Learn about Yahoo!:

Searching Yahoo! How to find stuff...	Suggesting a Site Help us build Yahoo!...
Browsing Yahoo! Just looking around...	Yahoo! Help Central Commonly asked questions...
Customizing Yahoo! Have it your way...	Yahoo! Features Browse our sites by topic...

AltaVista™ The most powerful and useful guide to the Net

Ask AltaVista™ a question. Or enter a few words in [any language ▾] Help - Advanced

Example: Where can I find free stuff online?

AltaVista™ **Help** AltaVista Home

Table of Contents

Basics

Advanced Help

Refine

Usenet

Add a Page

Frequently Asked Questions

The Basics

The AltaVista search service helps you find documents on the World Wide Web. Here's how it works. You tell the search service what you're looking for by typing in keywords, phrases, or questions in the search box. The search service responds by giving you a list of all the Web pages in our index relating to those topics. The most relevant content will appear at the top of your results.

A Quick Look at the Search Box

little time to look through, you will be repaid by greater efficiency in searching and better results.

Another useful port of call is your search engine's **Help** section. This will include specific instructions and advice on how better to use that particular search engine. The **Advanced Help** section can also be handy so don't be daunted by it. It doesn't mean that only advanced Internet users can use this section. It just means that the search engine can provide you with advice on how to improve your search if you are looking to do so.

A list of search engines you can try:

➥ **www.altavista.com**

➥ **www.yahoo.com**

➥ **www.excite.com**

➥ **www.hotbot.com**

➥ **www.infoseek.com**

➥ **www.lycos.com**

➥ **www.webcrawler.com**

Don't forget to see if these search engines have one that is country-specific. Using a specialist search engine will tend to restrict results to websites that are relevant to your own country.

Using Categories and Directories

Categories and **directories** are really one and the same thing: they are the varieties of topics that search engines have listed on their web pages. The topic headings act as links, so that clicking on one will reveal a further sub-directory and web pages on that particular topic.

With directories, all the hard search work has been done and the results are neatly categorised into topics. The big-

gest advantage of a directory is that it has been compiled by a human expert. This means that all the results will have been checked beforehand by this expert, who will make sure they are relevant, and that the contents of the selected websites are accurately described.

LookSmart, found at **www.looksmart.com** , is a good example of a directory.

Selecting one of the main categories will lead you to a further list of topics which will be related to the original category. This will help you to further narrow your search. You continue to do so by selecting from each sub-category list that appears until, after digging down further and further, you come to a list of websites that should be exactly what you are after.

At each step along the directory 'chain' you can always decide to change to a regular word search using the search engine. This means that you can either continue using the category selections or you can use the search box provided to type in a search word. Because you have already narrowed down the categories, using a search word at this stage will mean that the search engine will be searching through fewer and more useful websites.

❶ *Starting with a broad category, we have narrowed down our search to 2 suitable websites to look at.*

Directories are valuable because they start with very broad topic areas. This should help to point you in the right direction if you are stuck in your search attempts. In addition to the **www.looksmart.com** example above, you can find useful directories at the following web addresses:

➡ **www.yahoo.com**

➡ **www.webcrawler.com**

➡ **www.miningcompany.com**

Or try your favourite search engine.

Tip: Ask Jeeves

Ask Jeeves is your very own online butler who can be contacted at **www.askjeeves.com**. You use the Ask Jeeves web page just like any normal search engine. Ask Jeeves anything and he will return with suggested answers from many search engines. The benefit of Ask Jeeves is that you actually type in your search query like a question. For example: 'Where do I find the Statue of Liberty?' or 'How do I learn about bonsais?'

Keeping information

Ever come across a recipe on the Internet that you wanted a copy of? Have your children ever found an Internet picture that they want to add to a school assignment?

It is useful to know how to save information or a picture you come across when using the Internet. One way would be to bookmark the web page, as we have discussed on pages 43–7.

But what if the site changes or is updated? The identical information may not be there when you return in a week's or a month's time.

Another way to save a piece of text or an image from a website is to store it directly as a computer file.

How to save text

❶ Move the cursor to the start of the text that you wish to capture and hold down the left mouse button.

❶ *Hold down the left mouse button when the cursor is in position.*

ican REPUBLIC   ◀CUBA   BAHAMAS

A research vessel called *Quest* is sailing through the Caribbean right now, carrying scientists who hope to uncover the origins of Caribbean life or at least discover a few answers to the mysteries of biodiversity posed by this string of islands. The ship is carrying an Animal Planet film crew and a DCOL correspondent, who will report live from Navassa. Navassa is a tiny island where many species have yet to be identified and where scientists are discovering how new habitats may be born. Follow our live reports from Navassa and take a swing through the rest of The *Quest's* destinations to get a sneak peak at what you might discover on Animal Planet TV in 2000.

❷ Keeping the left mouse button pressed down, drag the mouse until all the text that you want to keep is highlighted. Then release the left mouse button.

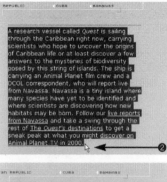

> ❷ *Drag the mouse down until you have selected the text you want.*

❸ Clicking the right mouse button (or using the **Edit** menu) you can either choose to **print** your selected text or you can choose to **copy** it.

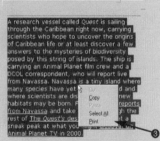

> ❸ *Clicking the right mouse button will bring up the option box*

❹ Copying text from the Internet is just the same as when you copy things within other computer programs such as word documents or spreadsheets. To copy the text, you should open up a new **word file** (or the equivalent) and transfer the text you have selected by using the **Paste** command. This text can then be saved within as a word document on a diskette or your PC.

❹ *The Paste function within the new word document will let you copy the text you highlighted from the Internet website.*

How to save a picture

① Move the cursor to the picture you
  want to save.

② Click the left mouse button. A small
  table of options will appear on your
  screen.

❸ Select the **Save Picture as . . .**
  option. Then save this image, as a
  picture file, directly in a folder on
  your computer. You'll be able to
  add this picture to letters you write
  or use it in school projects or any
  other work you may be doing.

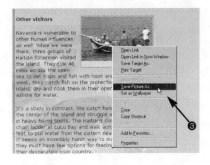

❸ *The right mouse button brings up the option
box which allows you to select the
Save Picture as . . . option.*

Thanks to the Discovery Channel (**www.discovery.com**) for these examples.

7
Improving *Email Skills*

Your email address book

There is no need to memorise or even write down the email addresses of your friends or family. They can easily be stored in your **email address book**.

An email address book is similar to any other address book. It is a place in which you can store the email details of your friends and family. This address book is a part of your email program, so all the addresses can be stored in your computer exactly where you want them.

All it takes is a little time to insert the names and email addresses of people you email regularly. Once this is done, when you want to email someone, you simply select their address from the address book and it will automatically be transferred to the address box on your email. There will be no need to type in the email address over and over again.

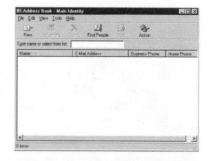

An empty email address book.

An example of an email address book with four addresses stored in it.

Get into the habit!

To start building up your email address book it is handy to remember to add an email address each time you receive an email from someone whose address you haven't yet stored in your address book.

When you are reading an email, think to yourself: *Do I have this email address?* If not, right-click on the incoming message and select the **Add Address** option to transfer the address to your address book automatically. Or you could add it to your address book manually.

A right mouse click on an incoming email will let you add that person's email address to your address book.

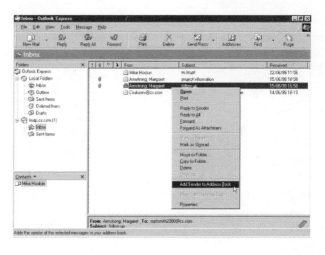

Selecting an email address by double-clicking your mouse button will automatically set up a blank email message with the recipient's details already entered.

Email fun

A fun way to send someone a greeting is to send them a special **email postcard**. It can be a lot more entertaining and personal than sending just a normal typed email message.

These special postcards are often fun pictures or photos that you personalise before emailing them to a friend or relative. You can even get email postcards with music or animations attached to them.

Egreetings and Bluemountain are recommended websites to visit to get your free email postcards.

Email postcards are especially useful for occasions like birthdays, Christmas or Easter because you can find postcards relevant for a specific occasion.

How do I find email postcards?

There are websites that specialise in having a selection of email postcards for you to choose from. They are also available to you free of charge. These sites are really good because you can select an email postcard, personalise it and sent it, all from the same website. You don't need to open up your email program at all.

Examples of where you can find free email postcards are:

www.egreetings.com and **www.bluemountain.com** .

How do I send an email postcard?

① Let's send a postcard from the **Egreetings** website. To get to the website, first type in the Egreetings web address on your browser's address bar.

Look down the list of categories to match the occasion you have in mind. Egreetings will present you with different email postcards that you can choose from.

② Once there, follow the instructions on how you can view the different post-cards or messages. Browse the range of email postcards and make a selection.

③ Follow the sending procedures which Egreetings makes very easy, by first entering the name of your recipient and then the personal message.

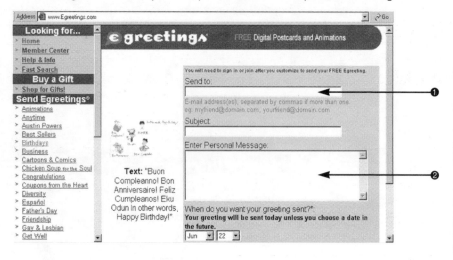

❶ *Enter the recipient's email address in this box.*
❷ *Your personal message goes in this box.*

Note that you will also be asked for your name and email address so that the recipient of your card knows who it is from.

④ Send the email and look forward to a reply.

Finding other free postcard websites

Some other websites where you can send fun email postcards:

Free postcards	Search

Email postcards	Search

Fun AND email	Search

Problem email

If, for some reason, an email doesn't get through to the recipient it will always be sent back to the sender. This is the same as getting a letter back in the post marked 'Return to Sender'. This type of problem is referred to as a **bounced email**.

There will be a message attached to your bounced email that will include the reason for your email not getting through. The most common one is that the email address doesn't exist and therefore cannot be found.

Example of an error message:

The message informs you that the recipient's name is not recognised.

This may mean that:

① You typed the address incorrectly, so check the spelling and punctuation of the address you entered. If you have made a mistake, then correct the error and resend the email.

② The domain or place responsible for the person's email is not working. Try again and if the same thing happens, you should contact the recipient and see if they are aware of any problem with their email server.

How to reply to an email

A great feature of email is that you don't have to bother with all the steps of sending an email from scratch if you reply immediately to an incoming message.

❶ *Click the **Reply** button on the tool bar.*

❷ *Or you can reply to a message by selecting the **Reply to Sender** option in the message menu.*

When you are reading the message on your screen you will see a **Reply** button. Alternatively, you can select the **Reply to email** option on the menu bar.

While the email message is still open, choosing one of the Reply options will automatically set up a reply email page for you. Your email program knows who sent you the original email and will automatically send the message back to that person. You simply type a reply message above the same email that you have just been reading. Then press Send.

Tip

If the message has been sent to other people besides you, selecting Reply will only send your email to the person who sent the message.

However, if you select the **Reply All** option then your reply email will be sent to everyone who received the original message. Remember, you can always check who your email will be going to, by looking in the address box before sending your message.

Forwarding an email

You can receive an email from one person and send this same email on to another person, without having to retype the message. To do this, select the **Forward** option on your email program. Then add the intended recipient's email address.

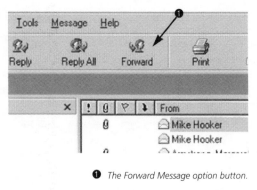

❶ *The Forward Message option button.*

You can either send the message as it is, or you can edit it or even add another message to it, before forwarding it by pressing Send.

Tip:
Do you work from home?

Anyone who works from home, at any time, will find it worth learning how to attach files to emails. You can work on files on your home PC and send them that day to someone back at the office or to a customer. There is no need to send a diskette through the post with your work on it.

Attaching files to your email

When sending an email it is also possible to attach a computer file to your message.

This will mean that the file you attach will turn up in the recipient's inbox along with the email message you sent. When you are a confident and regular user of email, you will find this an invaluable tool.

An **attachment** is a separate file that is sent alongside your email message. For example, you could send an email to a friend saying hello and also attach a copy of an assignment, or a saved picture file, or a spreadsheet you have been working on. Attaching files may be more common for work purposes. However, there are some good uses for it in the home.

How to attach a file

The process is very simple. Commands and option buttons will look different from computer to computer but the basic procedure is the same. Follow the step-by-step instructions below and in no time you'll be attaching files like a pro.

① Look for the **Attach File** or **Attachments** option on your email program.

The Attach button.

② Selecting the Attach File will then show your computer's **file manager**. The file manager is the directory of all the files on your computer and indicates which folders they are stored in.

③ Find the file that you want to send with your email. Select the file with a double mouse click or by using the **Add Attachment** button. Your email program will automatically copy this file and attach it to your email. Don't worry, the original copy of this file will not be altered in any way and will remain where it is on your computer.

From your list of computer files, select the file that you want to send as an attachment to an email.

④ Once the file is attached, send the email in the normal way. You might note in the email that you have attached a file.

Reading an email attachment

You might find yourself on the receiving end of an email with a file attached to it. You will know this because you will probably be informed about the attachment both by the person sending the email and by your email program.

You will be given the option by your email program of opening the attached file. To do so, select **Open File**. Or you could save it on to your computer and view it some other time.

One important requirement for viewing an attachment is that you must have the same software program as the attachment was created in. By this I mean that if a friend has sent you a spreadsheet created with the Excel spreadsheet program, then you will need to have an Excel spreadsheet program on your own computer in order to be able to look at, or modify, the attachment.

Your message screen will tell you if there is an attachment as part of an incoming email to you.

Coping with email overload

Setting up an **electronic filing cabinet** is the answer to sorting out an over-flowing email inbox.

If you want to keep a copy of an email someone sent you, it will cause problems if you leave it in your inbox after you have read it. Your inbox will start to overflow with old messages and it will be hard to tell which is an old email and which is a new one – especially if the whole family is receiving emails at the same address.

It is very easy to keep a copy of an email message in an electronic filing system.

It is a matter of first setting up your own electronic folders and then, when you have read a message, deciding either to delete it or save it under an appropriate folder.

Setting up an electronic filing cabinet

① Look in the File menu when you are in the email area. Select the **Folder** and then the **New** options as illustrated here.

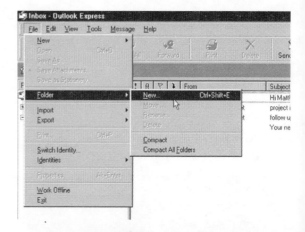

② When you have the **Create Folder** screen open, you then type in the name of the new folder that you want to create.

The Create Folder screen. It is up to you to give the folder a name.

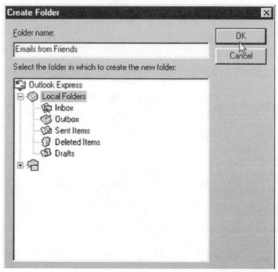

Adding an email to a folder

Once you have created a new folder it is handy to move read emails into that folder. This will mean that your email inbox will be clutter-free, and your saved emails well organised.

① After reading an email and deciding you want to save it, select the **Move to Folder . . .** option from the File menu. You will still have your email open on the screen.

Selecting the Move to Folder option from the File menu.

② The choice of folders will appear on your screen. Select the folder in which you would like to save the current email message. Click **OK**, and your message will then be saved in that folder.

Choose from the selection of folders the one in which you would like to store your current email and click OK.

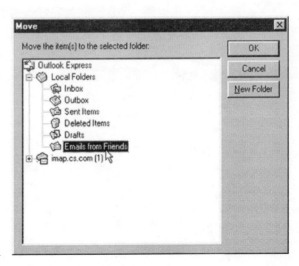

Email Security Check

■ When sending emails, remember that they can be read by other people. Don't send information that could cause harm to others or get you into trouble and don't write anything that may be damaging or embarrassing to you personally.

■ Think carefully before sending personal details to someone via an email if you are not certain who they are.

■ Sometimes an Internet shop or some other website may ask you to submit your personal details. Use your common sense. If it is a reputable company or website, then don't worry about filling in a personal form.

■ In general, don't send credit card details via email. Reputable Internet shopping sites ensure that credit card details are sent on a secure email line. (Learn more about this in the following chapter.)

■ If you have any doubts, make some more inquiries before sending personal information via an email message.

8
Internet_Shopping_

What is shopping on the Internet like?

The growing number of people who shop on the Internet do so primarily for three reasons. Firstly, it is convenient, then there are the great bargains and cost-savings, and finally, shopping on the Internet is FUN!

It's true that online shopping is becoming more and more popular. People are preferring to do their shopping in the comfort of their living room rather than battling with large crowds in stores. Some shoppers like the fact that Internet shops, or **online shops**, never close and will take orders twenty-four hours a day. I personally enjoy the large amount of choice that you have, which is all within a few clicks of the mouse.

Even if you are not a shopaholic, you may still find the thrill of an Internet auction or the ability to buy from a store as far away as Brazil both exciting and addictive.

Just browsing

You can just as easily window-shop on the Internet as you can in a real store. There is never any commitment to purchase if you visit an online shop. You are allowed to visit the shop's web page and look around to see what is on offer without having to spend a thing. This is especially ideal as it allows you to click between different online stores to compare prices and offers before you buy.

If you do plan a day's shopping in a real store, and have an idea what you want to buy, why not spend a few minutes on the Internet before you leave home? You can check how much things will cost you on the Internet, which you can then compare when you go into the store.

Is it cheaper to shop over the Internet?

You can't say categorically that shopping is cheaper on the Internet, but there are certainly lots of bargains to be had. Because many online stores don't have the same overheads as a real store, they can offer you the same products at a lower price, even when postage is included. Being able to compare prices of different online stores very easily and quickly should also help to save you some money.

Internet shopping saves you more than just money. It also saves you time and sometimes the frustration of having to trek around stores all day.

Shipping and handling

The most exciting part of shopping online is, of course, receiving your purchases. If you order products on the Internet, this will generally mean they will be delivered to you by post or courier.

A good piece of advice when ordering online is always to check what you will have to pay for shipping and handling. This is especially important if you are going to be buying something from another country and international postage rates will be involved.

Another hidden cost to watch out for if you are planning to purchase something from an overseas Internet store is the sales tax or customs and duty costs you may be required to pay when you get your goods delivered back. You may want to check what the potential import taxes are before purchasing anything from an overseas website.

Is shopping on the Internet secure?

There is a lot of talk about the Internet not being a safe place to shop. Most of this refers to the security issues of sending your credit card details over the Internet. As a result, some people do have concerns regarding online shopping and many have yet to shop over the Internet because of this worry.

If you are at all concerned, the first good news is that the large and reputable online stores guarantee that credit card details can be sent over the Internet safely and without worry. They have achieved this by ensuring that the connection between your computer and their online store is secure.

We will look at how this is done as well as suggesting other ways of making sure that your Internet shopping expedition is a safe one.

What is a secure website?

Sending an order for clothes or books or any other item across the Internet is like sending an email to the supplier. Because you have included credit card details, there is the possibility that someone could 'intercept' this email for fraudulent purposes.

Secure websites ensure that when you send this order form to a shop as an email, the information cannot be obtained by fraudsters – giving you protection and peace of mind.

Even in the highly unlikely event that you are a victim of online fraud, most credit card companies limit your liability to a nominal amount by law. Both the major credit card companies, Visa and Mastercard, tell customers that it is safe to shop on the web, although they do recommend you to shop at a website with secure servers. You may want to contact your credit card company and find out their policy for online Internet transactions.

How can I tell if my credit card details are safe?

So you have decided what you want to buy, you've filled out some personal details and then you are asked to enter your credit card number – is it safe?

Before entering in your credit card details with confidence, you need to run through a check to see if the website is secure.

Security check

Your browser will indicate whether the site that you are visiting is secure and whether the website uses the special techniques necessary to protect your credit card details.

The first thing to check is the **padlock** symbol on your web browser. You will find this symbol either on the browser toolbar at the top of your screen or it will be in the lower left or right corner of your screen.

Unlocked padlocks indicate that a website is NOT secure.
Locked padlocks indicate that a website is secure.

If the padlock is open, the website is NOT secure.

If the padlock is closed, you are entering a secure area. This means that the link between your computer and the website you are visiting is safe. You may also get a pop-up message on your screen telling you that you are entering a secure website.

Examples of messages that will appear on your computer screen when you enter a secure website:

Security Alert ☒

ℹ You are about to view pages over a secure connection.

Any information you exchange with this site cannot be viewed by anyone else on the Web.

☐ In the future, do not show this warning

[OK]   [More Info]

Security Information ☒

You have requested a secure document. The document and any information you send back are encrypted for privacy while in transit. For more information on security choose Document Information from the View menu.

☑ Show This Alert Next Time

[Continue]   [Cancel]

Note: The time to check for security is when you are at the checkout area of the website and are being asked to submit your credit card details. Don't be confused if the other web pages in the Internet website shop are not secure. Security on those pages is not required as you will not be using them to send your details, hence they will indicate an unlocked padlock.

Choose the right online store

Checklist

It is better to shop only at sites that you know are trustworthy companies, either because they are known to you personally or have been recommended in the press or by a friend. Here is a list of the things you should be looking for in an online shopping store:

① As many ways to contact the store as possible, including phone, fax, postal and email addresses. This will be helpful if you ever need to make an inquiry.

② What are the delivery details? How will you receive the goods and when? What will the postage and handling cost be?

③ What does the shop's website look like? If it looks professional and appealing, then the company has spent quite a bit of money designing the website. This should indicate that they are a genuine retailer and not a back-yard set-up.

④ Look for a returned goods policy. What is the company prepared to do if you would like to return your purchase? Will you receive a full refund? How many days do you have in which to return the goods?

⑤ Most sites should proudly acknowledge that they are a safe and secure website to shop on. This information is often reported in the Frequently Asked Questions area (FAQs). They will explain that they have secured their website with special credit card encryption services, making it safe for you to send your credit card details over an email.

How to shop on the Internet

Shopping on the Internet is as simple as looking through a website, adding the things you want to buy to an electronic **shopping basket** and proceeding to the website checkout.

 An electronic or online **shopping basket** helps you to keep track of the things you would like to buy. This makes it a lot easier when you plan to buy more than one item at a time. For example, if you would like to buy several compact discs most online stores will let you add your selections to a shopping basket as you select them. When you have finished you will

Tip: If in doubt, shop OFF the Internet

If you want to buy something from an online store but are still unsure about the security of its website, you will often have the choice of shopping OFF the Internet instead.

For example, the store may have a customer service phone number or fax number that you can call. Look for a link to the **Contact Us** web page on their website. This will have phone numbers or addresses where you can contact the store directly. So if you are uncertain, use the Internet to browse for products and compare prices, then purchase directly over the phone or fax, rather than submitting credit card details over the Internet.

be able to review what is in your shopping basket and the total cost of your purchases before proceeding to the checkout.

① First you must select an online store to visit. For this example I have chosen the large Internet book and music store, **www.amazon.com**.

When visiting an Internet shopping store, take your time browsing through the store by clicking back and forth between the web pages or use the automatic search tool.

❶ *The Amazon.com Home page – the place where we start our shopping! The automatic search tool helps you locate specific items quickly and easily.*

② When you find something that you would like to buy, select the exact item, colour or quantity that you require. Click **Add to Shopping Basket**. Your purchase will now be put into your electronic shopping basket.

Select more products if you wish and keep adding them to your shopping basket.

③ When you are ready to send the order to be processed, select **Proceed to Checkout** or **Review Basket**.
You will then have a chance to review the list of things you have chosen and see how much they will cost. You can remove any items at this point if you

❶ *After selecting a music CD, you add the item to your shopping basket.*

have decided that you don't want to buy them. Check that you have ordered correctly, and especially that you haven't made any typing errors. For example, you may want '12' bottles of wine, but not '121' bottles!

🛒 *Shopping Cart*

▶ *proceed to checkout*

Shopping Cart Items	Qty.
🎵 *Gold: Greatest Hits* Abba; **Audio CD** Usually ships in 24 hours	1

Make sure you check that the details of your purchase are correct.

Completing Your Order is Easy

We encourage you to enter your credit card number online (why this is safe). However, you also have the option of phoning us with the number after completing the order form. If you have any problems or questions, see the bottom of the page for details on our toll-free (800) customer support number.

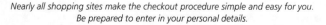

1. Welcome.

Please enter your e-mail address: |

Please check your e-mail address for accuracy; one small typo and we won't be able to communicate with you about your order.

○ I am a first-time customer. (You will be asked to create a password later on.)

○ I am a returning customer, and my password is |

Have you forgotten your password?

Nearly all shopping sites make the checkout procedure simple and easy for you.
Be prepared to enter in your personal details.

④ Then proceed with the website's particular checkout instructions. Most websites make these instructions very easy to understand. You will find that the information normally required will include personal details such as your email address and credit card details and a delivery address.

⑤ Having finished adding all your details, submit the order so that it can be processed and the goods delivered to you.

Confirmation of your order

Most online stores should send you a personal acknowledgement of your order. This will appear on your computer screen immediately to confirm that the order has been placed. You may also receive further confirmation by email.

Despite these records, you may also want to make a personal note of what you bought, and when, so that you are not surprised when it arrives on your doorstep a week later!

Major brands and labels

Have you got a favourite label or brand? Do you always buy the same make of cosmetics or the same brand of golf equipment or have a favourite clothes designer?

Then you should see if the company has a website. If they do, they might very well sell directly to the public through the Internet.

Why not try having a guess at the web address of well-known names or brands? For example, if you wanted Levi jeans, a good guess for their website would be **www.levis.com** . You might try **www.levis.co.uk** to get the UK website or **www.levis.com.au** for the Australian website. Alternatively you could try using the brand name as the actual keyword with a search engine.

Levi jeans	Search

Tip: Grocery shopping on the Internet

Why not order your weekly groceries on the Internet and have them delivered to your door? With some big supermarkets it is now becoming possible to order using the Internet. So if this interests you, why not try finding out whether your main supermarket has a website using the step above?

<Your Favourite Supermarket>	Search

Bargain-hunters

The web is a great place to try and grab a bargain. Shop for last-minute holiday offers or get top label clothes at discount prices. All it requires is a bit of time to search around the Internet for the best offers and to compare a few prices.

Bottomdollar and Bargain finder at the Shopguide website. Check them out.

Some shopping sites do the bargain-hunting for you. You enter the details of what you are looking for and they will search the Internet for the cheapest prices. The website will then report what the prices are and where you can purchase the item most cheaply.

www.bottom-dollar.com and **www.shopguide.co.uk/bargain finder** are both shopping search engines that will search for the best prices for you. The results that you get back from any search will link you to a web page where you can place an order.

Internet auctions

Fancy placing a bid for an old Elvis record or a holiday to the Caribbean? **Internet auctions** are becoming very popular with Internet shoppers. Firstly, because they are a great way to get bargains and secondly, because they are very exciting to be involved in. Wait to place your bid in an Internet auction, see the bid appear on the screen, and then feel your heart skip a beat when the bidding closes and you have been successful!

How auctions work

Internet auctions don't happen instantaneously like a normal auction, which is over in a matter of minutes. In an Internet auction the duration of the bidding lasts for a fixed period of time, which will be noted on the auction web page. Generally, the auction will either end in a few hours' or a few days' time. This means that you must enter your bid during this period and before the auction closes.

You can buy or 'bid' for nearly any product on auction sites. Most auction sites will provide a description and photo of the product or service that is to be sold. You should also know that you are generally buying from an individual who has put the item up for bid and not from the auction site itself.

Internet auctions are popular for second-hand goods as well. So if you are on the lookout for something new, make sure you are not bidding for a second-hand item without realising it.

Remember that although auctions are fun, they are also serious. If you enter a bid, you are entering into a legal contract. If your bid wins, you are obligated to buy that product for the agreed price. Bargain-hunters will love Internet auctions.

www.qxl.com and **www.ebay.com** are two very good auction websites. They are worth visiting just to see what Internet auctions are all about. If you are new to the Internet, go straight to the Help pages of these websites to find out more.

Ebay and QXL are two very good auction websites to look at. Both have very easy instructions for you to follow.

New auction sites are appearing all the time, so keep an eye open for one that might interest you. You might like the car auction sites, for example, or perhaps one that specialises in auctioning holidays.

You should also look out for auction sites that are based in your own country. This will obviously make the cost of delivery cheaper than buying at overseas auctions.

How do I find a shop?

If you are looking for a place to shop on the Internet, you will soon find that there are millions to choose from. Here are some suggestions for finding an Internet shop where you will be able to buy exactly what you want:

① Use a search engine

Type the item you wish to purchase into the search box. It might be a good idea to refine your searching (see 'Tips for improving a search', pages 52–7) by specifying the brand name or model and the country you would like to buy it from. Any search engine will give you a good selection of results to look at.

For example, if you wanted to buy wine using the Altavista search engine you could try the following searches:

Keyword: **Wine** – for a very general search

Keyword: **Internet wine stores** – for specifically trying to find wine sellers

AltaVista™	The most powerful and useful guide to the Net	
Ask AltaVista™ a question. Or enter a few words in	any language ▾	Help · Advanced
	wine	Search
Example: **Where is the sport cricket played?**		

Internet wine stores **[Search]**

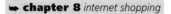

Keyword: **Wines stores AND UK** – for UK wine sellers only

| wine stores AND UK | Search |

Keyword: **French wine** – for suppliers of French wines

| french wine | Search |

② Search Engines them-
selves have their own
Internet shopping areas.
Look for the **shopping
link** on the search
engine's Home page. The
Internet shops will be
listed in a directory
format, making it easy to
track down a shop that
sells what you want.
Remember, though, that
all search engines will not
have the same shops, so
it may be worth looking
at the shopping direc-
tories of a few different
search engines.

Search engines have their own shopping areas you can browse in.

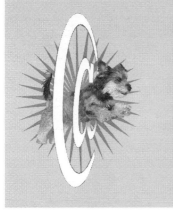

Tip: If you choose a country-specific search engine, then the online stores that are listed will be stores from that country. This means they will specialise in local delivery. For example, the **Yahoo! UK** website will promote UK Internet shops while the **Yahoo! Australia** website will list Australian sites.

After a while, you will soon build up a list of your favourite Internet shops, online shopping malls and auction sites (all of which you should bookmark, of course!).

Further hints and tips for Internet shopping

① Make sure you are getting the best price. Don't assume that because you have found something available to buy on the Internet it will be at the cheapest price. It pays to check other websites, as well as newspaper or magazine adverts, just to be sure.

② Print out and keep a copy of your completed order form before you send it. This will help to avoid problems arising over deliveries or payments.

③ Review your online order form before sending it. Ensure that you have typed everything correctly, including the quantity of goods you wanted.

④ If ordering from overseas, check any special specifications of the goods, such as electronics details or shoe-size measurements. Also check the extra VAT or shipping costs you may incur by bringing goods into the country.

⑤ If the product is expensive, see if you can get insurance coverage while it is in transit.

⑥ Finally, check off your Internet purchases from your monthly credit card statement, making sure that you agree with the cost of each one.

9
Internet *Travel*

Whether you travel regularly or you're planning a family holiday, the Internet is the perfect source of travel information for you.

Much of the hype surrounding travel and the Internet focuses on the cheap last-minute tickets that you can buy. While it is true that you can get fantastic holiday bargains this way, there are many other great ways to use the Internet for travellers. These include:

- Comparing the prices of airlines, travel agencies or holiday destinations.

- Booking hire cars, hotels or city tours in advance.

- Using email to communicate your arrival times to hotels, or to request that perfect room with water view!

- Researching your holiday destination, looking up historical facts or finding out about upcoming cultural events.

- Reading travellers' tales.

- Monitoring the weather for your holiday destination.

- Joining travel email clubs to communicate with other travellers, sharing stories, ideas and experiences.

- Bidding in an Internet auction for a holiday or for accommodation.

So even if you are an armchair traveller, the Internet is a great place to satisfy the travel bug!

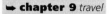

Get inspiration

Because the Internet is one vast reference library, it is bound to have information on almost any holiday destination you may be thinking of. Even if you just have a general interest in travel, it will be easy to spend a couple of hours reading about the experience of other travellers on the Internet, or looking up historical facts about a country or a place.

Most search engines or Internet Service Providers will have a 'travel' section segment on their web page. This is probably a good place to start

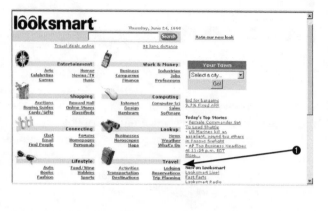

❶ The travel section on a typical search engine's Home page.

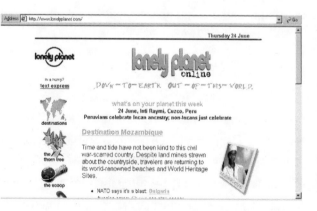

www.lonelyplanet.com – a comprehensive travel guide.

some general travel browsing.

No doubt you will come across a lot of advertisements and recommendations for Internet travel agencies or ticket sellers when starting your search here. You should also find plenty links to travel articles and general travel information to get you started.

Alternatively, if you want to get going right away and see what the Internet can offer travellers, then visit the sites illustrated on these two pages.

www.berlitz.com – for language tips and hints.

www.cntraveller.co.uk – a link to the Conde Nast Traveller magazine.

Planning your holiday

If you are thinking of a particular holiday destination, the Internet is always a good place to gather information and look at the travel options available to you.

To explore the whole range of tourist information such as travel arrangements, air fares, accommodation and weather reports, the search engines should be your first port of call. If you have a specific country or city in mind, then you may want to try the following typical searches:

<your destination> AND travel	Search

<your destination> AND hotels	Search

<your destination> AND weather	Search

<your destination> AND tourist information	Search

Alternatively, you may be interested in an activity holiday but not yet certain of your destination. In this case you may want to enter a search such as:

<your hobby> AND holidays	Search

<your hobby> AND travel	Search

When using a search engine, remember that you can be as general or as specific as you like in conducting the search. The examples above will direct you to general travel websites through which to plan your holiday. But let's suppose you have seen an attractive resort in a holiday brochure – then there may be a chance that the resort has its own website.

You could try searching for the resort's website in order to make contact with them directly by using keywords such as:

<resort name> AND <destination>	Search

If you do find the website, it is bound to offer more information on the resort than a holiday brochure would contain. It will probably also give the email address, enabling you to ask for more information or to check prices and room availability.

Tip: Whatever good websites you come across, don't forget either to bookmark the website or save the information in a file (see pages 63–5) so you can find it easily when you want to book your holiday or are ready to take off!

Buying tickets or booking accommodation

Buying tickets

If you have a credit card, you can use the Internet to book tickets or accommodation there and then. Or you may prefer to use the Internet to window-shop for the best bargains and check availability before booking with a travel agency over the telephone.

The websites of most of the Internet tickets sellers are linked to the same seat allocation systems as travel agencies. This means that you can just as easily confirm seat availability on the Internet as you can through your local travel agent.

The airlines themselves are starting to offer flight sales on their own websites. You can now book a flight directly on the British Airways website

British Airways is just one of the airlines allowing you to book flights directly from their website.

(**www.british-airways.com**) and use your credit card to pay for it. The airline Qantas (**www.qantas.com.au**) provides the same service.

When purchasing tickets or a holiday from a website, make sure you are dealing with a reputable company. Better still, check if the website is a member of an official body such as ABTA (Association of British Travel Agents). Of course, all the other rules for Internet shopping also apply: ensure that the website is secure when sending credit card details and make sure you get further contact details of the company in case you need to contact them later with a query.

Booking accommodation

If you are a more independent-minded traveller and like making your own holiday arrangements, then the Internet will make it a lot easier for you to conduct some research into local accommodation.

Try these searches:

<your destination> AND hotels	**Search**

<your destination> AND campsites	**Search**

With a large variety of type and quality of accommodation now available in most cities and countries through the Internet, a web search similar to the examples shown on the next page should give you quite a few accommodation websites to look at.

For example, a search for 'Paris AND Hotels' resulted in the following list of websites:

> ▸ **AltaVista found 6,206,050 Web pages for you.**

1. Paris Hotels: Millennium Copthorne Luxury Hotels and Resorts:
Millennium Commo
    Paris Hotels: Millennium Copthorne Luxury Hotels and Resorts:
    Millennium Commodore Paris, Paris,...
    URL: www.mill-cop.com/pages/c/comcope.html
    Last modified 28-Jan-99 - page size 3K - in English [Translate]

2. Libertel Hotels Paris
    Hotels in Paris, France. Accommodations in Paris. Cheap
    accommodation in Paris. Browse through our list of hotels in...
    URL: www.turquoise.co.uk/Paris/LibertelHotelsParis.htm
    Last modified 6-Jun-99 - page size 4K - in English [Translate]

3. Hotels in Paris- HOTELS & RESIDENCES DU ROY - FRENCH HOTEL
GROUP -
    Hotels in Paris, France. Accommodations in Paris. Cheap accommodation in Paris. Browse
    through our list of hotels in...
    URL: www.hotel-california-paris.com/dhtml/hrr1.html
    Last modified 27-May-99 - page size 5K - in English [Translate]

4. Hotels in Paris, France- HOTELS & RESIDENCES DU ROY - FRENCH HOTEL GROUP -
    Hotels in Paris, France. Accommodations in Paris. Accommodation in Paris. Browse through our
    list of hotels in...

Recognising that many people will soon be using the Internet to find travel accommodation, hotels have started adding photographs of rooms, location maps and price lists to their websites. This allows you to make up your own mind about where you would like to stay, just by visiting the website. Typically, the hotel will also provide an email address, making it equally easy for you to check on room availability. Just send an email!

An example of a hotel's website.

Travel bargains

The best travel or holiday deals are generally scooped up at the last minute. These bargains occur when airlines or tour operators release special offers to try and fill seats or accommodation that would otherwise go empty.

You can still visit a travel agent or call an airline directly to get these last-minute bargains but I think it is much easier to see and choose from the selection offered on the Internet. Travel companies can put information on to the Internet very quickly and without the expense of printing brochures or posters. This means that you will find the most up-to-date holiday bargains on the Internet.

Some websites actually specialise in promoting nothing but last-minute airfares or holiday packages. The company **Cheapflights**, found at **www.cheapflights.co.uk** , is a good example of a UK discount travel website.

To find other website travel agencies and special offers, try the following keyword searches in your favourite search engine:

cheap flights	**Search**

bargain holidays	**Search**

last minute holidays	**Search**

Tip: Bid for a holiday!

Auction sites are a good way to get a bargain holiday. You may have to be a little flexible as to your destination or holiday dates. However, seeing the holidays which are currently being auctioned on the Internet might just inspire you to go somewhere you hadn't even considered! For Internet auctions, see pages 93–5.

Visit a tourist office before you go

Don't wait until you arrive in a country to visit the tourist information office.
Connect to the Internet beforehand and visit it. Even if the website of the tourist office isn't great, at least you will get a mail address or phone number to contact to get more information sent to you.

Most major destinations will have a tourist

The Canadian Tourist Office website is just one of the many official tourist office websites that travellers can visit before they leave for their holidays.

information website on the Internet. You could try searching for this yourself or you might find it at the **Tourism Worldwide Directory** at **www.mbnet.mb.ca/lucas/travel/tourism-offices.html** . Or try searching:

| <your destination> AND tourist office | Search |

If it is country-specific information that you are seeking I can highly recommend the **World Travel Guides** found at **www.travel-guides.com** . You will get lots of in-depth information on almost all countries on this website so it is ideal for pre-adventure holiday research.

Tip: Not sure of what the local currency rate is for your holiday destination? Then visit the Internet **Currency Converter**, at **www.xe.net/currency/** , so that you can work out how much your money will be worth in the country you are visiting.

10
Weekend *Internet*

The Sunday newspapers

There is no longer any need to go down to the news-stand to pick up a copy of your favourite newspaper. Read it on the Internet.

Because the Internet is all about sharing information, it is not surprising that the big newspapers have established their own websites or that with their expertise in bringing you the printed news, these websites often give you the most up-to-date information across all websites on the Internet. They are also a good source of weather news, so you can check what sort of weather is expected for that weekend barbecue you are planning!

The Paperboy provides links to numerous newspaper and magazine websites.

How to find your favourite newspaper on the Internet

Next time you are reading a printed copy of the newspaper, look on the front page or in the editorial column to see if the website is advertised.

Alternatively, ask the **Paperboy** to help you find it. The Paperboy, found at **www.thepaperboy.com** , is a great website that provides links to all the major newspapers as well as to some popular magazines.

Foreign news

Practising another language? Have a friend who lives in another country? Planning a business trip or holiday overseas? If you ever need to keep up with the news, weather or the language of another country, you may find visiting that country's national newspaper website handy. Plus, using the Internet, there is no need for expensive foreign subscriptions. For links to foreign newspapers, visit World Wide News (**www.worldwidenews.com**) or try the website addresses of the following foreign newspapers:

➡ **www.nytimes.com (USA)**

➡ **www.lastampa.it (Italy)**

➡ **www.lemonde.fr (France)**

Movies and entertainment

The weekend means rest and relaxation. More often than not, this will involve watching a TV film or video or sometimes going to a cinema, show or concert.

The first unmissable benefit of the Internet for movie-goers is the huge amount of online film reviews, opinions and facts. The choice of websites is enormous, ranging from those of the big studios right down to amateur movie critics, all of which will offer you personal comments and opinion.

Most new films these days have a website made as part of the pre-release movie promotion. Advertisements or poster billboards for the movie will display the website address. So if you cannot wait for a film to be released, you can visit the website for sneak previews, photos and behind-the-scenes gossip.

If you are looking for general reviews and movie gossip there are some really good dedicated movie sites that specialise in nothing else but film-related information. The Internet **Movie Database**, found at **www.imdb.com** , is probably the best. Not only does it have all the latest gossip and reviews but it also has an inbuilt search engine that helps you trawl through the vaults of movie information, past and present. You could also try **Hollywood Online** at **www.hollywood.com** .

Tip: You can find previews of all the upcoming movies at the websites of the individual film studios. Here is a list of the major ones:

➡ **Twentieth Century-Fox www.foxmovies.com**

➡ **Disney www.disney.com**

➡ **MGM www.mgmua.com**

➡ **Paramount www.paramount.com**

➡ **Warner Brothers www.movies.warnerbros.com**

Booking cinema or theatre tickets

Most major cinemas have their own websites these days. These will contain information on what is showing where, location of cinemas, screening times, and often an online ticket-ordering service. Reserving tickets on the Internet is a lot more convenient than waiting in a queue at the cinema. If you cannot find a cinema's website yourself, you can contact them directly and ask for their web address. Once you have this, make sure you bookmark it.

If you want to book tickets to the latest shows and concerts, **Ticketmaster** is probably your best stop. This website will have a comprehensive list of the latest shows, reviews, ticket prices and ticket-ordering facilities. Visit Ticketmaster UK (**www.ticketmaster.co.uk**) for all concerts and shows in the UK. Or visit the Australian Ticketmaster website (**www.ticketmaster.com.au**) for concerts and shows in Australia.

Weekend sport

The weekend also means sport for many people, either participating themselves or watching it on television. The Internet will not replace the feeling of direct participation. However, it can offer you information on how to improve your game, put you in touch with clubs or sporting events or bring you the latest results from your favourite team.

A search on sport with a search engine will flood you with relevant sporting websites to look at. These will range from the large professional and dedicated sports websites to the homemade website of a sports enthusiast. All will be able to offer you something unique, depending on what you are after.

General – **www.express-sport.com**
Golf – **www.golf.com**
Football – **www.football365.com**
Rugby – **www.scrum.com**
Formula 1 – **www.itv-f1.com**
American Sports – **www.cnnsi.com**

If you are looking for more active involvement than just catching up with reading the latest sporting news and reviews, why not participate in an Internet **chat** room dedicated to your favourite sport? This will let you swap comments with other sports lovers from all over the world. See Chapter 12 *Chatting on the Internet*, to learn how easy it is to join in with a chat area.

Alternatively you could join an email club and receive a regular email on a sports topic of your choice. See the following chapter on email clubs, or go straight to **www.onelist.com** for a listing of sports-related email clubs.

Personal finance

The weekend is a good time to catch up on your personal finances. Unfortunately it is also the time when your bank, your building society, your insurance company or mortgage broker is closed.

However, it is becoming more and more common for financial institutions to offer a 24-hour service on the Internet. This means you can sort out your finances from home instead of queuing at the bank or phoning around for the cheapest insurance rates.

Here is a list of personal finance activities that can be handled through the Internet:

- Personal banking
- Applying for credit cards
- Searching for personal loans
- Finding all types of insurance cover
- Arranging pensions and life assurance plans
- Paying regular bills
- Monitoring stock prices and buying or selling shares
- Seeking free financial advice from experts

How do you go about finding these services?
It will take time to be comfortable with using the Internet to undertake personal finance activities, especially as most of us like the security of a face-to-face

meeting or phone conversation when dealing with financial matters.

The first point of call may well be your existing bank. You could inquire whether they have any form of Internet banking available as an extension to the current services they provide. If not, you can always check with the other main banks and think about changing accounts if necessary. Similarly, most large building societies and insurance companies are now starting to offer online customer services.

Useful search techniques

When it comes to finding competitive interest rates on credit card or car loans, all your search knowledge and the following tips should help you:

Firstly, it would be easier to use a search engine that specialised in websites from your own country because this will direct you to financial institutions that operate there. For example, **www.yahoo.co.uk** if you're a UK resident or **www.yahoo.com.au** if you live in Australia.

Next, it is a matter of searching for keywords to find relevant websites. For example:

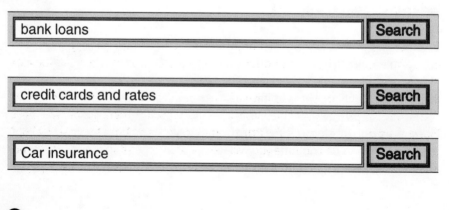

Tips:

Look out for advertising banners on the Internet to direct you to relevant financial websites.

The financial institutions invest quite a lot of money on Internet and **online banner** advertising. If you are attracted by a banner advertisement on your screen, clicking on it will take you to the advertiser's website.

Let's say you conduct a search for the word *Insurance*. Don't be surprised if there is an online banner advert from a large insurance company on the results page. This could provide you with a useful link to an Internet insurance company.

What's for dinner?

Whether you are an aspiring chef or just need a great recipe to keep the family happy, the Internet has lots to offer you – the most obvious being the millions of free recipes available to help you add a zing to your weekend meals.

Just think how handy it is to have all these recipes to choose from, especially if you have a printer available. Visit a recipe website, then, when you have found a tempting recipe, use the **Print** command on your browser or select Print from the File menu. In no time you will have a hard copy of the recipe from the Internet to take with you into the kitchen and because it is just a piece of paper

Recipe Exchange, found at
www.recipexchange.com ,
has lots of recipes to search
through.

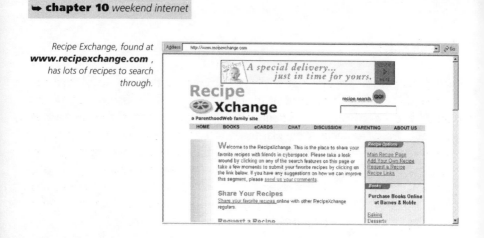

there is no need to worry about spilling anything on it as you would a recipe
book.

A general search using the keyword *Recipes* will bring you lots of food-related
and recipe websites. Being a bit smarter with your search by now, you will soon
find just the recipe you are looking for. Here are some examples:

| recipes AND barbecues | Search |

| recipes AND chinese | Search |

| vegetarian recipes | Search |

Gardening

Even if you prefer to spend your weekends in the garden, don't forget that the Internet also has much to offer. With many gardening enthusiasts using the Internet and a large number of dedicated gardening websites, you can always find advice on what needs to be planted when, or how to trim that hedge.

If you fancy yourself as a bit of an expert in a particular area of gardening, why not join a gardening email list and contribute answers to people's gardening questions? Or, if the weather puts a stop to your weekend gardening plans, you can still read up on some gardening skills on the Internet or participate in a gardening chat room (see Chapter 12 *Chatting on the Internet*).

Gardening advice	Search

Gardening AND roses	Search

Gardening AND chat room	Search

Tip: Still bored?

If you are really stuck for something to do on the Internet, why not find out what everyone else is doing?

There are websites that specialise in listing the top-visited web pages across the Internet. They record how many people go to these websites over a day or a week and will then post the results with direct links to these top-ranked websites.

These are a great place to get inspiration from. You can be sure that you are going to visit some very good websites because everyone else recommends them.

➡ **www.hot100.com**

➡ **www.top50.co.uk**

➡ **www.web100.com**

11
Email *Clubs*

Email clubs are a great way to contact and keep in touch with people who share your own interests or hobbies. Email clubs are also referred to as **email lists** because in practice an email club is a large list of people who send and receive emails on a given topic. Rather than sending individual emails, one main email is sent to everyone on the list.

It is up to you to track down an email list that you are interested in. Next, you will need to submit your email address to the club or list of your choice. This process is often called **subscribing** to the email list. Once a subscriber, you will receive the group email on a regular basis until you decide otherwise.

But that is not all. You can also participate by sending your thoughts or opinions to be included in the group email that everyone will receive.

Why join an email list?

The purpose of a mailing list is to share news, stories and advice on any topic you like. It is nice to receive a daily or weekly email from like-minded people who enjoy the same interests as you. You might have to join a number of email lists before you find one that you really enjoy reading and contributing to.

Reading regular emails about a hobby, over a cup of coffee, is a good way to start the day. So give it a go!

How to join an email list

The email list is the electronic headquarters of the email club. To join it, you will need to send an email to the list subscription area, requesting that you are put on the email list. You will also need to send your email address so that the club knows where to send you the group email. Everyone who receives the group email has their email address stored on the email list.

Onelist, found at **www.onelist.com** , is a website that makes subscribing to a mailing list really easy. This website has hundreds of email clubs easily arranged for you to browse and select from. It also provides clear instructions on how to sign up to the mailing lists.

A search in the music category, for example, reveals further classification of lists

The Onelist website – your one-stop shop to sign up to an email list that interests you.
A handy website tour found towards the bottom of the first web page will explain all you need to know.

by music type and year. Browse these sub-categories to pinpoint your specific interest.

The benefit of a website like Onelist is that they summarise the content of each email list on their website. They even state whether or not these are safe for children to join. To sign up to an email list, simply double click on the one that you choose.

Types of email lists

Find a Mailing List	Home | Sign-off
Music	
40s (18 lists)	Instruments (246 lists)
50s (32 lists)	Jazz (120 lists)
60s (195 lists)	Latin (85 lists)
70s (95 lists)	Lyrics (103 lists)
80s (148 lists)	MC/DJ (95 lists)
90s (748 lists)	Metal (842 lists)
Acoustic Guitar (72 lists)	MIDI (104 lists)
Alternative (1251 lists)	Musicals (98 lists)

Keep all members of Active Ingredient informed of what is going on.

AlbanyDMBers [English] [Safe for Kids]
Going to see DMB on Dec. 5th, 1998? join for more specific chat about the show

alfonso1000 [Hebrew] [For People Over 17]
A damn cool list

AllThatJazz [English] [For People Over 10]
A list about jazz music, all jazz artists, like Metheny, Steely Dan, Coltrane, Davis, Marsalis, etc. etc. and groups with a jazzy touch, like Jamiroquai and Dave Matthews Band.

Double-click on the email club that you want to join.

Closed or open email lists

Some email lists that you join will only be one-way emails. That is, they are set up to provide regular information or news for you, but they don't enable you to contribute to the email. This is called a **closed** email list.

Other lists that you join will encourage you to send in your opinion about a current topic. Or you might email a reply to a question that was posted on the group email. This communal, information-sharing email list is called an **open** email list. Of course you are not obliged to contribute, but the option is there if you want to.

Unmoderated or moderated email lists

Some lists may be uncensored or **unmoderated**. This means that any message posted by a member of the list will be added to the group email, even if the message is irrelevant to the topic or offensive in content.

Moderated email lists, on the other hand, have a person who edits the members' contributions, organises them and compiles the group email. As a result, the email that you get sent each time is probably more relevant and unlikely to include offensive matter. For this reason a moderated email list will give you a better quality of email reading.

What happens if you don't like the email list?

All emails sent to you from an email list indicate how you can stop receiving the group email. Generally you **unsubscribe** in the same way as you subscribed, by sending an email to the email list headquarters. The email you send will indicate that you wish to unsubscribe from the email list. Once your preference has been logged you will no longer receive the group email.

Instructions on how to unsubscribe from an email list will be included in the initial welcome message email – so keep a copy of that for future reference.

Sometimes you may find that you just haven't got time to read the group emails although you don't want to quit the email list altogether. If you are in this situation you could either save the emails in a folder to be read at the weekend

Tip: Going on holiday or going away for a while? If this is the case, your group email will still keep being sent to you. This will start overcrowding your inbox. Unless you really want to come home to a backlog of emails, I would suggest that you temporarily un-subscribe from the email list and then resubscribe on your return from holiday.

or at a later date (see pages 77–9) or just delete them from your mailbox without reading them.

Search words

Some search words to help you find more email lists to join on the Internet:

E mail clubs	Search

E mail lists	Search

mailing lists AND <your hobby>	Search

12
Chatting *on the Internet*

What is Internet Chat?

Internet chat, or just **chat**, is another way to communicate on the Internet.

Chat is an exciting and fast-paced way to communicate and it is a very popular Internet activity. You might think the word 'chat' implies speaking to people and it is not far from it. Chat in fact involves typing brief messages that other people read and respond to instantaneously. It is similar to email but messages are sent and read immediately. Another way to describe it is to think of chat as passing small written notes back and forth to someone across the Internet.

The big appeal of chat stems from it being instantaneous, and the fact that it occurs between a whole variety of people, living all around the world.

You don't need to be an expert to partic-ipate. To get involved in chat, you only need to enter a chat room on the Internet. A

A typical chat website. This is the type of thing you will see when you are participating in a chat room.

chat room is just a special web page. Once you visit one of these web pages, or *visit the chat room*, you watch the messages that are getting posted back and forth among the chat participants. You can simply watch the flow of messages, or, if you are adventurous, you may want to add a message of your own.

Most chat areas on the Internet offer different chat rooms for numerous different topics. You can find chat rooms for discussing news, sports, books, films and romance. This way, you can find a chat room to talk about your favourite hobby, discuss a movie you have seen or debate the latest sporting results. Alternatively, there are general chat rooms where you can talk about anything you feel like. Chat rooms are also places to meet new people from around the world.

Note to parents: It is common for some chat rooms to be adult in nature, so care should be taken if younger members of the household want to participate in chat. I would recommend supervision for this.

How to chat

To chat on the Internet you need to follow these steps:

① Find a chat area

②   Register with a chat service
③   Select a chat room
④   Understand the chat room
⑤   Start chatting!

①   Finding a chat area or chat service.

This is a special website that sets up and arranges different chat rooms for people

to meet in, on the Internet. There are quite a few good chat areas to choose from. The choice is yours.

  A chat service should be offered by your own Internet Service Provider so you could start here. Alternatively, you may want to try one you find elsewhere on the Internet. Most search engines offer a chat service these days.

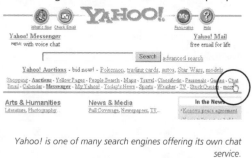

Yahoo! is one of many search engines offering its own chat service.

  For the following example, I will use a very popular chat area from **Yahoo!** Find this directly from the web address **http://chat.yahoo.com** or look for the keyword *Chat* on the Yahoo! Home page (**www.yahoo.com**).

②   Registering with a chat service

You have to register in order to enter a chat room. Because you are a new user of the Yahoo! Chat area you should select the **Sign Me Up** option in order to do so. You are then asked to answer a few questions on an online form, including your name, where you are from, and your email address.

You don't have to use your real name; in fact most people like to use a nickname or fake name when chatting. Remember, though, that this means the people you come across in a chat room may also be using a false name or false profile.

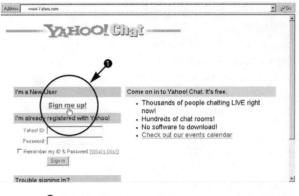

❶ *Select the Sign Me Up option as a new user of this chat area.*

When completing any chat registration form, note that not all the questions need to be answered. You may feel comfortable just filling in the compulsory questions and leaving the others blank.

③ Selecting a chat room

Okay, we have registered ourselves with Yahoo! Chat, so now we

Note that not all questions on the registration form are mandatory.

want to start chatting. The next step is to select which chat room we would like to enter.

Yahoo! gives you a large selection to choose from. You will either be able to select a room based on your interest or hobby; otherwise, if you don't want to chat about anything in particular, select 'general chat'.

You have a large selection of chat rooms to choose from so you are sure to find one to suit you.

Once you have made your choice, select the **Start Chatting** option. This will take you straight to the chat room if you are not already there.

④   Understanding the chat room

One thing to note about chat areas is that they require a bit more time to access than a normal web page. This is because special programs are required to make a chat room what it is. These take time to start. So be a little more patient than usual while you wait for the chat web page to appear.

A typical chat room will look like the one below.

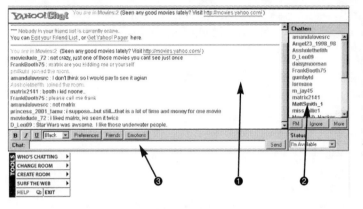

The chat room as it appears on your computer screen.
❶ *The stream of messages*
❷ *The visitors' box*
❸ *The message box where you first type a message before sending it to the chat room.*

Tip for beginners:

Upon entering the chat room, you will find that you have joined in the middle of a conversation. If this is your first visit I suggest you just watch the chat before participating. This will let you pick up the thread of the conversation. If there are many participants in the chat room, you may find that there is more than one conversation going on!

The actual 'chat' involves people sending a constant stream of small messages to each other. These messages will scroll down in the chat screen. The name of the person or, in this case, the Yahoo! user name, will appear on the chat screen before each message. There is also a visitors' box, which indicates the number and the names of the participants currently in the room.

⑤ Start chatting!

You have been watching the conversation long enough – now it is your turn to send a brief message. All the messages that you send need to be typed in the blank **message box**. After typing your message, send it to the chat screen by pressing Return or Send.

Why not start by typing '*Hello room*' in the blank message box? Your message will appear on the screen as part of the ongoing chat dialogue. Don't be surprised when people say hello back to you!

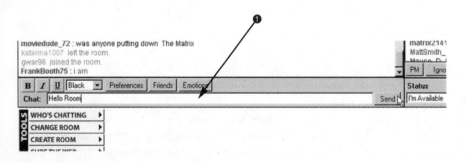

❶ *Type your messages in the blank message box before pressing Send which will post your message for all the room to see.*

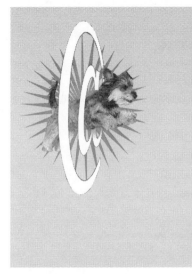

Tip:
Changing chat rooms

All chat areas on the Internet will let you change rooms whenever you like. There is no need to stay in a room. The **Change Room** option will be made clear to you. So if you are finding a chat room not quite what you are looking for, try a new one.

Special chat language

It is perfectly natural to feel slow and awkward when you first join in a conversation in a chat room. It can take time to get into the full swing of things. One particular thing that can cause some confusion for first-time chat users is understanding **chat language**.

Chatting is quite fast and messages are typed, not spoken. Because of this, a unique form of shorthand has developed that allows chatters to communicate quickly and effectively without having to spend time typing long messages. This language takes a while to understand. To help you, here is a list of basic terms.

Tip:
Chat Language

A/S/L – age, sex, location
e.g. A/S/L is asked as a question to find out a chat-room member's name, if they are male or female and where they are from in the world.

LOL – laugh out loud
e.g. someone makes a joke and then you may type 'LOL' in response to signal that you laughed at the joke.

BRB – be right back
e.g. informs the chat room that you are briefly away from your computer, perhaps making a cup of coffee.

TYVM – thank you very much
(G) – grinning   **(S)** – smiling   **(J)** – joking

People also communicate their feelings to a chat room. The basic and most common 'smileys' are:

:-) smile or happy   :-(frown or unhappy   ;-) winking   :-o surprised

If you see an abbreviation or a 'smiley' in a chat room and you don't know what it stands for – don't be afraid to ask. Chat-room participants are a social lot and will be quite happy to explain the meaning.

Chat-room checklist

■ Chat is like any other form of communication. Be polite and friendly and you will get the same response back. Ignore any person who is being abusive or offensive.

■ It is always best to write in lower case. In chat rooms, writing in capitals is like SHOUTING AT SOMEONE!

■ Remember that the message you send is seen by the whole room.

■ Chat is anonymous, so anyone can pretend to be someone they are not.

■ Don't give personal information out to strangers, especially your address or contact or credit card details.

■ If you ever feel uncomfortable in a chat room, simply join another room.

■ Many people go to a chat room just to watch. If you just want to watch, try choosing a large room with lots of participants – it will be more fun.

Most importantly

■ If you leave a room and have been chatting with people, don't forget to say goodbye to them.

Sending a personal message

When you are in a chat room with many participants you can also send a **personal message** to a particular person. This is a one-to-one message that only they will be able to see on their screen. Likewise, someone could choose to send a personal message that only you are able to see.

The term 'personal message' is often abbreviated to '**PM**' in chat-room language.

To send a personal message, first select a participant with whom you would like to start a private conversation. It might be someone who has just mentioned that they are from the same home town as you, or they may share your hobby. For whatever reason, you want to direct a specific question or greeting to them.

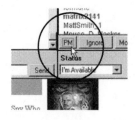

Click on the PM button or select their name directly by a double mouse click. This will bring up a separate, one-to-one chat room and empty message box. A message typed in this box will appear as an identical private box on the recipient's screen.

The blank private message box appears on your computer screen when you want to send a message only to one person and not to the whole chat room. Type in your message in the blank message box as you would when sending a message to the whole chat room.

Chat with celebrities

The big and popular chat services often invite famous celebrities to chat with the public on the Internet. This means that you are invited to join a chat room that has been specifically set up for participants to ask the celebrity questions or send a message to them across the Internet.

Because these chats are live, they will have to be scheduled by the chat service for certain times. So keep a look-out on the bulletin board of your chat service to see if there are any upcoming celebrity chats that interest you. Or why not contact your chat service directly and suggest that they arrange a chat event with your favourite celebrity?

Where to find chat rooms

It shouldn't be too difficult to find a chat room to get you going, as discussed earlier in this chapter. If you want to experiment and try out more than one chat area, here are some suggestions for finding others:

– First check to see if you ISP offers chat rooms.

– See if your favourite web search engine offers a chat service.

– Visit the **Hot 100** website at **www.100hot.com** . They have an updated list of the Internet's most popular chat rooms.

– Try these search words:

| Chat | Search |

| Chat websites | Search |

| Chat websites AND <Your country> | Search |

| Chat websites AND <Yourhobby> | Search |

13
Internet Advice
for Parents

This section offers help to parents to ensure that the time their children spend on the Internet is safe, enjoyable and productive. By being aware of both the benefits and the potential dangers of the Internet as a parent, you will be better equipped to provide guidance for your children when it is their turn to use the Internet. You will also want to make sure that they enjoy the very best the Internet has to offer them.

Becoming an Internet parent

It is often the case that children catch on to things quicker than their parents. The Internet is no exception. Often children are the first in their family to use the Internet, being introduced to it at school, as well as experimenting with the Internet on the home computer. It can be a very exciting place for children. The possibilities for learning and communicating across international borders are a fantastic educational opportunity for young people.

There are concerns, raised by parents, about children being involved with the Internet. With limited censorship on Internet content, allowing a ten-year-old to access the Internet can seem a dangerous prospect, especially without supervision. Others are concerned that if children spend too many hours on the Internet as well as watching television or playing video games, there won't be enough time left for homework or outdoor activities.

When the Internet is used at home, it is really up to the parent to ensure that as well as having fun, a child is involved in useful and safe activities when browsing the web.

The Internet is like television

As a parent, you would recommend certain television programmes for your child to watch and not allow them to watch others. The same rules should apply to the Internet. Don't ban the Internet altogether. Instead, look for positive and specific websites for kids and teenagers.

Encourage your children to visit these suitable websites. Bookmark them in a special area which can be easily located by your children. This chapter will point

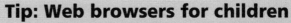

Tip: Web browsers for children

Using the Internet can be a lot more fun for children if they use a special web browser especially designed for them.

Surfmonkey is a web browser that has been made especially for kids. With its very own helpful onscreen monkey and a computer screen that looks like a rocket ship control panel, it is probably going to be a lot more fun to use than an adult Internet browser.

If you are a parent, it is nice to know that Surf-monkey also makes it *safe* for kids to search the Internet. Each site will automatically be checked for safety and suitability of content before a child is able to connect to that website.

You can get Surfmonkey directly by downloading it from the **www.surfmonkey.com** website. Easy instructions on the website will show you how to do this.

you in the right direction of some websites for children that are both safe and fun to visit.

Benefits of the Internet for children

The Internet and computer-related activities are becoming another *must have* skill for children. So it is great to see children embrace new technology as a fun activity, rather than a chore. Having the Internet at home can give your children a valuable head start in understanding and using the Internet. Here is a list of some of the benefits of the Internet at home:

- It allows you to spend more time with your child and be involved in their education.
- It helps children learn skills such as problem-solving, computer awareness, information-gathering.
- It is a world of learning that complements schooling, books and home life.
- It opens up the world to a child. They are no longer restricted in when, how and whom they can visit. Geographical boundaries don't exist on the Internet.
- It also builds a desire in children to learn for themselves.

What are the potential dangers of the Internet?

The open and uncensored nature of the Internet also means that there can be potential dangers for young users. However, with proper guidance, these dangers can be avoided and as a parent you can ensure that all Internet experiences are positive. Some key areas to keep in mind:

- Offensive material and content can be found in all areas of the Internet, not just on web pages. This type of material could also find its way into emails or chat-group sessions.
- The Internet is used to meet and contact people. For obvious reasons this can cause problems, especially because people can easily pretend to be someone they are not. Children can be a lot more naïve in these circumstances. In

Internet chat rooms, for example, it is more common to use a false name than a real one.

– Advertising has now got a hold of the Internet. Blinking signs and flashing banners can make things very appealing to purchase, especially to young shoppers!

– The need to balance children's activities. It is a good idea to limit the time that

The Yahooligans search engine for kids.

Tip:
Search engine for kids

A search engine is always a popular way to get started on the Internet. For children, it is best if they start with a search engine that has been specially designed to cater for their needs.

Yahoo!, for example, has a specifically tailored Internet search engine for children. The Yahooligans search engine is found at **www.yahooligans.com** .

Another good search engine for children is **Ask Jeeves for Kids**, found at **www.askjeevesforkids.com** . Ask Jeeves is an online butler who will help them find anything they want. The best thing about this search engine is that instead of typing in a search word, they ask Jeeves specific questions, such as 'Where can I learn more about horses?' or 'How good is Michael Jordan?'

*Type in direct questions to the **Ask Jeeves the answer** box.*

children spend on the Internet so that they have sufficient time left for home-work and to pursue other interests.

Help for parents to stay in control

Like most parents, you probably have rules about how your children should deal with strangers, what films they are allowed to see, how long they can spend playing video games or what shops they can go into. Many parents have found that if they apply similar rules to their children's use of the Internet, this can help to alleviate parental anxiety.

Rules for meeting people on the Internet

As you will know by now, there are many ways that you can meet people via the Internet. There is email, email clubs, email pen pals or chat rooms. Most people you meet on the Internet, just like those in the street, are decent people enjoying the Internet as much as you are. However, there can be the occasional rude or mean person on the Internet too, so here is a list of some good **do's** and **don't's** for you to pass on to your children:

■ **Don't** give anyone you meet on the Internet any personal information (name, address, phone number) unless your parent says it is okay.

■ **Don't** share your Internet password with anyone, not even a best friend.

■ **Do** ask your parents' permission to use your credit card online.

■ If you decide to meet an Internet friend in real life – **do** arrange to meet in a public place and under your parents' supervision.

■ **Do** ignore any email or other message that you or they feel is strange or confusing.

■ **Don't** use bad language on the Internet.

■ **Do** always be yourself when on the Internet and don't pretend to be anyone or anything you are not.

Better still, you could help your children to find someone suitable for them to send emails to or communicate with on the Internet, like an email pen pal for instance.

Tip: Email pen pals

There is nothing like the thrill of receiving a letter from a pen pal from the other side of the world. Having a pen pal can be really interesting. Children can swap stories, talk about their family, their school, their pets, where they live, absolutely anything. It can be a lot of fun for them.

Having a pen pal these days doesn't require you to lick a stamp or wait for a letter to come halfway across the world. You can write and send messages to your pen pal using email. I suppose that means you become *email-pals*!

Pen Pal Box is a good website to start with to find a pen pal for your children to send emails to. Following the easy instructions on the website, you can search for pen pals that are the same age as your children; a picture of their flag will tell you what country they are from. The web address is a little tricky but worth remembering –

One place to go to find email pen pals.

www.ks-connection.org/penpal/penpal.html – because Pen Pal Box is a highly recommended website.

Don't forget you can always use search engines to help you look for pen pal websites for your children.

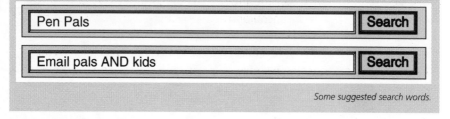

| Pen Pals | Search |
| Email pals AND kids | Search |

Some suggested search words.

Set some house rules

Unfortunately, because of insufficient censorship, the Internet does contain material that is too explicit for children to view. It is also unfortunate that without trying too hard when browsing the Internet, children could easily come across obscene material. A good set of **House Internet Rules** can help avoid some of these dangers.

Here are some common-sense ideas that you can use as the basis for House Internet Rules in your home:

① Get your child to ask for permission before using the Internet. This will allow you to supervise them. A close parental eye on the computer screen when your child is exploring the Internet can ensure they are viewing appropriate websites and content.

② It is important to make sure your child understands what is off-limits for them to look at. This is made easier by encouraging them to visit all the sites that are safe, fun and educational. This chapter ends with a list of great sites for kids to visit.

③ Think about setting times and time-limits on how long your child can use the Internet for. An alarm clock may come in handy in this case.

④ Involve the whole family in the Internet. Putting the computer in a family room is a good start. It will encourage everyone to use the Internet in a sensible way.

⑤ You could check with your child's school how they monitor children's Internet use and activity. This may give you some ideas and guidelines for home use.

Help with kids' homework

The Internet can be a great help with homework or school projects. With the Internet, children have a massive reference library at their fingertips. They are no longer limited to the information they can get from their local or school library to help them with schoolwork or a class assignment. And since they can look for information from all over the world, they are sure to get a top class mark! Here are a few tips as to how you can help them:

Looking for information

① Start with a favourite search engine.

② What is the topic of the assignment? Type in the search word box the topic of the assignment. For example, the project may be on *blue whales*.

Blue whales	**Search**

③ Let's assume that the search didn't give you many good websites to look at and you still need help with the project. Don't give up. Try the search again but this time try some other words that might be associated with *blue whales*. For example, try searching:

| marine mammals | Search |

| sea creatures | Search |

If, on the other hand, you found too many results, you may want to narrow your searching. So try again, using some more advanced search techniques. Try:

| Blue whales AND habitat | Search |

| whales AND eating habits | Search |

Saving the information

You will find lots of information on the Internet to help children with their projects. The next step is to know how to make a copy of this information to help them write their school assignment.

If you come across any interesting or relevant information, just print each web page when you are reading it. Use the Print button on the web browser or select

Print from the File menu.

You can also copy the information directly on to a **word file**. Select the information, or paragraph, that you would like to save. Highlight the text with your cursor by clicking and holding the left mouse button until the area you want to copy is highlighted.

From the **Edit** menu, select the **Copy** function. Then, after opening up a new **word document**, paste the text on to the blank word document where you can save and retrieve it later.

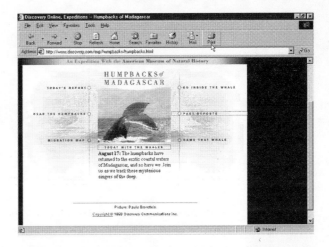

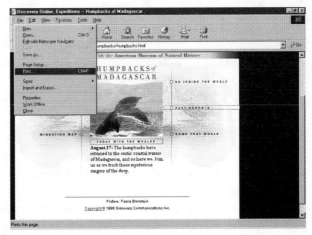

SINGING
Male humpbacks sing songs made up of short groups of sounds, sometimes while hovering alone about 50 feet below the surface, flippers stretched out, heads down, and tail-flukes pointing up toward the surface.

BLOWING or SPOUTING
As whales breathe at the surface of the water, they explosively exhale clouds of water droplets from their blowholes – the nostrils on the tops of their heads. These clouds of water are called the spouts or the blows.

SPYHOPPING
A whale rises slowly straight up out of the water to poke its head just above the surface, as if to have a look around, before sinking back into its more usual horizontal position.

KICKFEEDING
The humpback splashes water with its flukes, stunning nearby fish. The whale dives, then returns to the surface, its mouth wide open for a meal. This is another feeding behavior and, thus, not expected to be observed off of

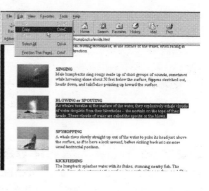

❶ *Select the area of information with your cursor and by dragging with the mouse.*

Of course you should remind your children that the project must be their own work and not a copy of someone else's – including someone else's web page!

Handy websites for school projects

While using a search engine will give you loads of websites to get information from, these are three really good ones that your children may find helpful for school projects.

■ The **Smithsonian Institute**, found at **www.si.edu** , has a massive collection of links and sites for them to look for information. There is even a link for the Encyclopedia Smithsonian.

■ The **Internet Public Library** provides library services to the Internet. Find the website at **www.ipl.org**.

■ A personal favourite is the **Discovery Channel** website at **www.discovery.com** . Not only would this be useful for school projects, it is worth visiting at any time because it is so interesting.

Electronic help for parents

There are many software and Internet programs that help you, as a parent, filter out unwanted web pages from the Internet. These programs can be installed on to your computer and act as a supervising parent, even when you are not around. The programs are designed to block access to sites featuring adult content and censored material. This type of electronic help can be obtained from numerous sources.

First check your Internet Service Provider to see if they have already incorporated **Parental Controls** in the service they offer you. Large service providers pride themselves on their provision of Parental Controls. A quick call to the customer service centre may help you locate various ways and means to restrict children's access to explicit web page and Internet information.

Next, you could visit a computer or software store where many child supervision computer programs can be purchased off the shelf. A visit to the store may also help because the shop assistant can explain the different options available to parents and how you instal the program on your computer.

Finally, there is help for parents on the Internet itself. Some websites make available child supervision programs that you get directly off their site. If you are uncertain how to get software programs directly from the Internet, find someone who can help you or take time to follow the very easy onscreen instructions. Sites offering this type of help include:

These websites are worth visiting to find electronic help to monitor what your children see on the Internet. Alternatively, visit your local computer store for good advice.

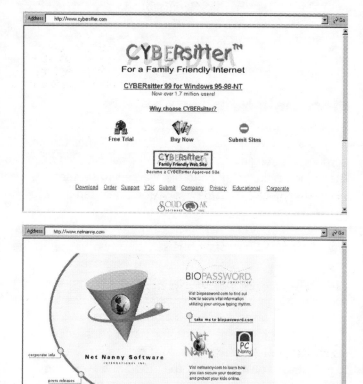

➡ **www.cybersitter.com**

➡ **www.netnanny.com**

➡ **www.cyberpatrol.com**

Websites for kids

Here is a list of suitable websites for children. But remember, half the fun of the Internet is letting kids find their own fun websites to visit and share with their friends.

➥ **www.kids-space.org**

➥ **www.launchsite.org**

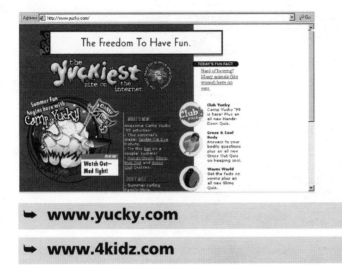

Address http://www.yucky.com/ ▾ Go

The Freedom To Have Fun.

the **Yuckiest** site on the internet

Summer Fun begins here with Camp Yucky

Watch Out— Mad fight!

Club Yucky

WHAT'S NEW
- Awesome Camp Yucky '99 activities!
- This summer's craze! Spider Tik Lite t-shirts.
- Try this hat on a coupla' suckers! - Hands-Down Slimy, Bug Out and Gross Out Quizzes.

DON'T MISS
- Summer surfing

➤ TODAY'S FUN FACT
Hard of hearing? Many animals (like worms) have no ears.

Club Yucky
Camp Yucky '99 is here! Plus an all new Hands-Down Quiz.

Gross & Cool Body
Answers to your bodily questions plus an all new Gross Out Quiz on keeping cool.

Worm World
Get the Facts on worms plus an all new Slimy Quiz.

➥ **www.yucky.com**

➥ **www.4kidz.com**

➥ **www.ebig.com**

➥ **www.everythingcool.com**

➥ **www.disney.com**

➥ **www.kids.warnerbros.com**

➥ **www.coloring.com**

➥ **www.beakman.com**

Index

Notes

Sent Messages folder stores copies of
sent messages if you click "Save Outgoing Message"
"Find message" on vertical navigation bar
under COOL TOOLS

MULL - IONA
WWW. ANTOR. COM

Welcome to Isle of Mull & Isle of Iona

Oban & Lorne & Argyll

Places to Go — Island

Isle of Mull

Welcome to Isle of Mull & Isle of Iona

Notes

Sandie! - themacleods@xtra.co.nz
Rattra@farmersweekly.net

HUB (Edinburgh Festival).
www.hubtickets.co.uk
E.mail: boxoffice@hubtickets.co.uk
Hub Ticket Patron no. 455409

www.scotlandspeople.gov.uk
User name: limab.ll@aol.com
Password 31P1SMJW

www.nls.uk/maps

Uniform Research Locator = URL.

See Teach Yourself - p. 78 et seq.

➡ **favourite websites**

Favourite Websites

www.yahoo.com
www.excite.co.uk
http://infoseek.go.com
http://webcrawler.com
http://www.altavista.com
http://www.yell.co.uk   (Yellow Pages)
https://www.v1v.co.uk
http://www.Hotmail.com
www.homeinternetchannel.com
www.looksmart.com
www.searchuk.com
www.ukplus.co.uk
www.yahoo.com
www.yahoo.co.uk
www.hotelselect.co.uk
www.trailfinders.com
www.flight-offers.co.uk
www.visitscotland.com
www.go-fly.com
www.enjoyment.co.uk
www.qas.org.uk
www.oddbins.com
    macpal@lux-hotels.com (Makedonia Palace)
www.nfumutual.co.uk
www.nfus.org.uk

www.freechurch.org.

www.eif.co.uk
www.RCAHMS.gov.uk   (Historical Society)

www. DukeshillHam. co. uk

Favourite Websites

Fiona Sime   mutt-jeff@shaw.ca

http://www.interdynamic.net

www. ANTOR.com   — for UK tourist boards.

Plan de Calidad Hotelera de Tenerife

www. scan. org. uk — Scottish Archives

www. nls. uk/pont

www. scran. ac. uk
        edina. ac. uk/statacc   ⎫ MAPS.

www. old-maps. co. uk

www. aaparking. co. uk/winter

www. capitalsearch. co. uk   (genealogy)

www. scotairways. com · To London City

flybe.com —   To London City.

easyJet.com —   To Gatwick

go-fly. com .   To Stansted.

~~Scottish Life Archive~~

165

martyn @ sjmackay. fsnet. co. uk

01383- 732057
Dial up number for FREESERVE
ANY TIME
www. brsc. com
08089916001

Email Addresses

martyn @ sjm

martyn 90 @ Hotmail. com   (Peruvian 2)
- cathie. ross 2 @ sympatico. ca
- Kirsty @ orbiter. co. uk
- willie @ orbiter. co. uk
  Sax @ ENSORS. co. uk
  IPS @ ENSORS. co. uk
- william. cruickshanks @ uk gateway. net. (Kattra)
  sheilaross
  SRoss @ Lynx. org   (Sheila)
- sandra macleod @ compuserve. com
- X fiona macleod Fiona @ Hotmail. com
- Rsime @ mb sympatico. ca   (Russ)
  audrey. mackay @ lineone. net

  Jeannine Grant :- grantaland @ mantraonline. com
  Rsime @ shaw. ca
  http: // www. orbiter. co. uk / house
      "   "   "   "   / Porsche
  Colinmackay @ CS com
- sheila @ brsc com   (Sheila)
  Catriona Mackay @ CS com
  Maarten Westerdunk : fmcw @ online. no
  martyn 90 @ Hotmail. com
  Password   Peruvian 2
  Secret question : Mother's first name
  Answer   Rachel.

— COLINMARK1 @ aol. com
— CATRIONABALDRICK @ aol. com

John.Torrie @ Charles - Stanley.co.uk

Willi :-   http://www.orbiter.co.uk/emma1/

Email Addresses

WMM :-   limabill @ aol.com

SCOTLAND ONLINE/TRAVEL.COM   (Flights)

www.
MAARTEN "—— fmcwe@dial.pipex.com
http://www.planetis.net/uk

www.interdynamic.net
www.google.co.uk
yell.com/motoring/buying a car/where buy.

reservations @ saga.co.uk

Rascal 48 @ Hotmail.com - Angela
                        → bellnet.ca
Sheila.Ross: dragons @ ~~inetsmic.com~~ - Home
                sheila @ bvsc.com

www.bridgeinn.com   - RATHO.
~~info~~ www.malcolmlochhead.com

www.dunfermline.net
Sheilagreer @ aol.com
david @ overskibo.freeserve.co.uk
↑ sime @ mts.net
www.orbiter.co.uk/maldives

stachjer @ netvision.net.il
www.malcolmlochhead.com.

167

New AOL phone access
0808 - 990 - 9000

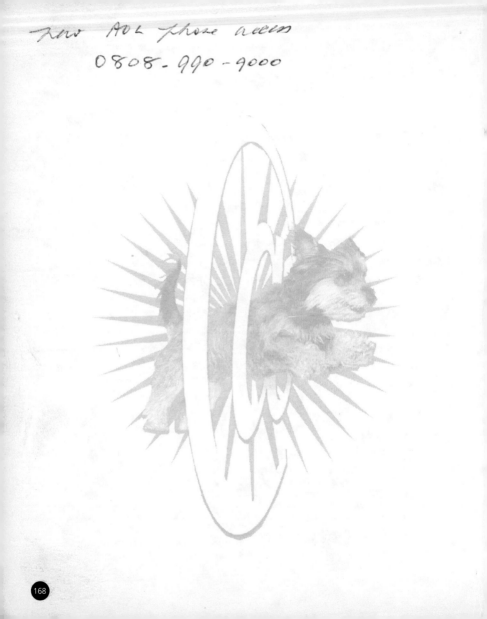

732057

Call 0800· 2796771 Member Services

0808-994-4001 - Access co failed to respond.
Access via this no not available

0808·990 9000
0808-993·3048
0808-991·6037
0808-991-5037

0800 - 376-4407 - Options for
Cancellations

0800 - 376-1324 / 0800 - 376- 7444   Option 2

Option 3.

Change the price plan back to.
    normal telephone line connection.

0800 - 376 - 7444.   Option 3.   X 2456

AOL Live Help.

0800 - 376 - 4407 Option 3 then option 2.
    Cancellation